The Ordinary God

About the Author

Hilary Wakeman is a founder member of the Open Christianity Network of Ireland. A retired member of the Church of Ireland clergy, she is the author of *Saving Christianity: New Thinking for Old Beliefs* (The Liffey Press). She lives in Schull, Co Cork.

THE ORDINARY GOD

Notes from the Far West of Ireland

Hilary Wakeman

The Liffey Press

Published by
The Liffey Press
Ashbrook House, 10 Main Street
Raheny, Dublin 5, Ireland
www.theliffeypress.com

A catalogue record of this book is
available from the British Library.

ISBN 978-1-905785-73-5

The essays in this book originally appeared in the *Southern
Star* newspaper, except for the last three which appeared
in the 'Rite and Reason' column of *The Irish Times*, and are
hereby reprinted with permission.

Printed in the Republic of Ireland by Gemini International.

CONTENTS

Introduction

A bible discussion group, parishioners of various ages, was getting tied up in knots on a rather basic subject, God.

In frustration, one woman said to another, 'But – what sort of God are you talking about?'

The other woman looked puzzled. 'Just the ordinary God,' she said.

I liked that. The ordinary, everyday God. The take-for-granted God. Whether we're 'religious' or non-believers, maybe we spend too much time wondering what sort of God we're talking about, instead of simply getting on with relating to the 'God' that I believe comes instinctively to most of us. If we've had a religious education, from schools or parents, we may need to drop a lot of stuff that has been drilled into us. If what we think we know about God doesn't feel good, or doesn't feel true, then it probably isn't good and isn't true. Like love, this is a subject where we do better to trust our gut feelings.

The articles in this book come largely from that point of view. Most of them appeared in the *Southern Star* newspaper over a two-year period beginning in September 2007. They were written for the ordinary people of West Cork, a people for whose down-to-earth-ness I have had a huge respect since coming here in 1996 as the rector of the furthest south-west parish of the Church of Ireland. What West

Cork people really think about things is often learned from what they choose not to say, but must be read non-verbally.

These articles were written for Catholics and Protestants and the people in-between and outside, for anyone who is interested in the difference between religion and spirituality, or in what our churches are doing or not doing or might do in the future.

The final three articles were published in the *Irish Times'* 'Rite & Reason' column.

I am grateful for the friends who have commented on these pieces and to the strangers who have stopped me in the street to talk about them. And especially to my husband John and other members of my family who have put up with having the pieces tried out on them before publication.

Hilary Wakeman
September 2009
Schull

I

It's Good to Talk – Especially about Religion

The author maintains that with religion, change and growth are inevitable. If a thing isn't growing, it's dead. And the biggest area of change is belief.
[8 September 2007]

Religion is fascinating. There would hardly be a man or woman in Ireland who does not have some sort of opinion about it. It is a huge part of our history. In recent years it has gone through a low time, with falling numbers in our churches, and pessimists predicting the end of Christianity. But now it seems that what has been happening is something that has happened all through the centuries. And that is – change. We are curving gradually into some sort of change.

We don't see change when we look back. We imagine that the Church and the faith have been changeless from the very beginning. Yet much of the particular piety and religious practices that we think absolutely basic have only been around for a couple of hundred years or less. The Christianity of the 1960s, for example, in Ireland or England, Rome or America, would be barely recognisable by a seventeenth century person.

Change, for some people, is exciting, while to others it may be threatening. But change and growth are inevitable. If a thing isn't growing it's dead. And instead of pretending change isn't happening, wouldn't it be better and healthier and altogether wiser to be talking about it? What this column hopes to do over the next few months is to look at a wide range of matters concerning Christian faith, belief, religious practice, and the part that all our churches and denominations play in the community. It will be looking especially at areas of change. And one of the biggest of these is belief.

When our belief in God hits the rocks it can be very frightening, especially if we don't feel we can talk to anyone about it. It can happen when someone we love dies – 'Why did God allow that, didn't I pray hard enough?' Or when we see the results of a natural disaster – 'What sort of God would let that happen to innocent people?' Yet these sort of reactions come out of ideas of God that were skewed in the first place. Or we start thinking about God and religion and suddenly it doesn't seem to make sense any more, and we wonder why we didn't see that years ago. Or, sometimes, it all just seems to fade away over time, because it has stopped being real to us, and we are left feeling a bit lost, a bit empty. In these cases what we could really do with is other people, people to talk with, people who will be honest with us about their own thinking.

What doesn't help is sweeping it under the mat. All those people in church on Saturday evening, or Sunday morning – what's going on inside their heads? Sure, many of them will be contentedly being in touch with God. But a good number of others will be wondering what they're doing there when they 'don't believe a word of it', as a well-known novelist said on the radio recently. 'I love going to church,' she said, 'I love the words and the music and all that, but I don't believe a word of it.' Someone else has coined the phrase 'non-believing Christians' who, they say, are increasing greatly in number. If this is so, why aren't we talking about it? Why are we all pretending that our faith is 100% rock-solid nineteenth century stuff? What changes do we need to make to allow ourselves to continue with integrity as Christians, with all the goodness that brings?

And we can look at our churches and the way they are organised. That could be something we want to talk about. Maybe we feel the decision-making is still all done at the top. Maybe we wonder whether Jesus would have wept if he had foreseen all these vast institutional structures and hierarchies. Where there is a falling in the number of vocations to priesthood or ministry, perhaps we should be letting fresh air into our thinking about the way the ministry of the church is managed. Like asking whether having one full-time clergy person is the ideal way of helping a community relate to God, or whether there are other ways. And looking at what women bring to ministry. The Methodist church is doing interesting things now, with training a wide range of people for lay ministry.

Bad things have been done in the name of religion, and lives have been ruined by those bad things. All the more reason, then, for our churches to work with their undoubted gifts of healing, for individuals and communities. Survey after survey shows that people who consider themselves religious are happier and live longer. That can't be bad. But how do we help ourselves and others to discover or rediscover that trust in God – or whatever other name we give to 'the ground of our being' – which sets us free from our own narrowness? How do we learn to experience the reality of that 'God' not as a second-hand acquisition, something we've been taught about, but first-hand, for ourselves?

In many places, particularly in urban areas, new forms of worship are attracting the younger people that so many of our churches say they have lost. This column will try to explore some of these, and work out what their appeal is – and whether this sort of experience is likely to spread. It will look at the impact on churchgoers of practices such as meditation and yoga, pilgrimage and labyrinth-walking. It will also look at what the churches are doing about justice and creation issues, such as poverty, immigration, health, ethics, fair trade, climate change, ecology. It will be asking people whether they think we can ever expect to see all our denominations and traditions come together into one unified Christian church. And it will be asking, also, whether Ireland has gone too far down the tiger road of materialism, or whether it can turn again and become the microcosm of the Kingdom of God that our saints and scholars were liable, on a good day, to think it.

Best of all would be if it could encourage people everywhere to be talking with each other about their own views on religion, their own hopes and concerns.

2

Keeping the Churches Alive All Week Long

The author believes that our churches need to be more welcoming. They should involve people in all sorts of events and groups seven days a week. [6 October 2007]

One of the pleasures of being a retired member of the clergy is that you are free to go to church services anywhere you want. One Sunday, when I hadn't been able to get to my local church in the morning, I remembered seeing a notice on a church building in a nearby village. 'Sunday Service, 8.00 pm', it had said. 'Yes,' I thought. 'I'll go there.' I arrived ten minutes early, and waited in the car expecting to see people going in. No-one went in, no-one came out. No sign of life there at all. At five past eight I gave up and drove home again. Obviously 'Sunday service, 8.00 pm' didn't mean every Sunday. Only the Sundays that the regulars knew about.

That was a Methodist church, as it happened. But are the others any better at communicating a welcome? In other parts of Ireland I have seen Church of Ireland buildings with padlocks on iron gates set in heavy railings. I'm sure the parishioners don't mean it, but the message it gives is, 'Keep out, this is ours.' Or simply, 'This place is dead.' C of I churches are good at having notice boards, though, with the times of services and the name or names of the clergy.

There's a splendidly colourful one in Clonakilty. Catholic churches, on the other hand, almost never have notice boards. The message that gives is, 'Ah, everyone knows when Mass is, and who the priest is and where you can find him.' Pity the poor visitors on their holidays.

Shopkeepers know that their buildings have to look inviting and welcoming if they are to attract customers in. Why should it be different for churches? That was the issue looked at recently by the Church of Ireland in this diocese. A paper called 'Church Buildings – a Tool for Mission?' was presented to the Diocesan Synod by clergywoman Eileen Cremin. In it she points out that many people will think twice about entering a church if they have had a bad impression of the exterior. What was good enough 100 years ago, or even 30 years ago, is inadequate 'to do the work of God in the changed context of a pluralist society,' she says. It's not just a matter of people expecting kitchens and toilets. We need to be creative about our buildings. And to do that we must be able to cope with change, even though change can be painful. 'Creativity will not happen if we spend precious time clinging on to things or old habits that hamper our ability to be people with a mission.' The starting point, she says, is to ask God and ourselves, 'What is the mission of our church in this context?' Prayer, then planning, then preparation – 'and don't forget to make friends with your local heritage officer!'

I went to see Eileen Cremin in her Fermoy parish, where she has responsibility for five church buildings. It's clear that she thinks a one-day-a-week church is a waste. Seven-day churches, she thinks, can give something to the community, involving people in all sorts of events and groups. Simply having the church open to all, every day from morning till dark, can be good. And sometimes, she says, you have to do something interesting instead of just waiting for people to come. She likes the idea of an all-Ireland 'open churches day' once a year, encouraging people to look into buildings they may never have entered before. Then, if the inside of those buildings are warm, and attractive, and even beautiful, those people may return and may eventually become part of the worshipping community. People need beauty, Eileen says, and we get to know God through our senses. 'We need to recognise the powerful part which our buildings can play in bringing about transformation, which is at the heart of the Gospel.'

If your church building looks dark, cold and uninviting, says the website www.getyourchurchnoticed.com, 'it may suggest that your church is unwelcoming, even if the reality is that your congregation is incredibly warm and friendly!' If the exterior is giving the wrong message, it says, think about the entrance. 'Do you have heavy, wooden doors that people have to negotiate before getting in? You'd be surprised how much of a 'Keep Out' message that communicates to those unused to coming to church. What about replacing them with glass doors, so people can see what's happening inside? Or how about replacing your entire entrance with an open, light, airy foyer that looks welcoming? What about putting comfy seats, pot plants, a bookshop or even a coffee shop in that foyer? It's no coincidence that many major firms use precisely these methods to make visitors feel welcome.' That website is connected with a book, *100 Ways to Get Your Church Noticed*, published by Kingsway. Both are full of

good information and ideas about communication, dealing
with notice boards, posters, magazines, and media-liaison –
but also buildings.

Sometimes the real problem can be that people love their
church as it is and don't want it changed. Richard Giles has
written a beautiful book called *Re-pitching the Tent*. The work
of proclaiming the living God, he says, 'is undermined and re-
pudiated by buildings which speak of a geriatric God incarcer-
ated in an old folks' home.' He mentions a small church which
shone with the effects of tender loving care, but was 'a de-
lightful evocation of times past, with very little connection to
life as we know it. A harmless pastime for anyone so inclined,
but nothing more.' Yet even old churches, he says, can and
should be de-cluttered. Because space, like silence, is restful
and can bring us into the presence of God.

Sadly, clergy are mostly untrained for the management of
change, Giles thinks, and unprepared for 'how vicious people
can become when their church-museum is threatened with
"desecration".' Like Eileen Cremin, he believes churches should
be alive all week long, bases for social action, workshops,
classes, offices, places where the kettle is always on the boil. All
giving people 'reasons to come in and out, and excuses to pop
into the place of assembly for a moment of prayer'.

But even where there is a desire to bring a church building into the present age, change can cost a lot of money. I
asked Eileen if there were inexpensive ways that a community could brighten up its building. 'Keep it clean!' was her
swift answer, mentioning a church building she had seen
where some wonderful woodwork was sadly thick with
dust. And make the grounds nice, she added. She talked

about one graveyard where the parishioners got rid of the weeds and the fallen trees, and cleared around the tombstones, and everyone who came there after that said how beautiful it all looked. Work like that doesn't cost money.

It's all about communication. Many years ago, in France, I was impressed by the cross-shaped notice boards at the entrance to every village. They gave the Sunday Mass times in that place. I guess that sort of thing might be too much to hope for, here, and now. But that was real communication!

3

Praying to the God of the Parking Spaces

The author believes that there is some truth to the Hindu concept of 'karma' – good and bad fortune being related to good and bad acts [3 November 2007]

One day when I was driving into Skibbereen I realised I had a few minutes to spare, and that I could call in to one of the shops for something I wanted. But it wasn't urgent, and I didn't have time to go into one of the big car parks. So I'd only do it if I found a convenient curbside parking place. All the old clichés about praying for a parking space came into my head, and I resisted the idea. If God grants trivial requests for parking spaces, what sort of God is God if serious prayers – for someone's life to be saved, say – are not granted? No, I would not pray for a parking space, I thought. That would be a wrong sort of idea about God.

I turned a corner, and there was a parking space. Not just any old space, but outside the shop I wanted to go to. I think I'd say I was stunned. Was someone trying to tell me something? But of course, it was a plain coincidence. Of course it was. But was it? An elderly parishioner of mine used to talk about 'godincidences'. I think this was a godincidence. Whatever about it, when I recovered from the shock, I laughed with pleasure and offered thanks.

Some people might say it was to do with the Hindu concept of 'karma'. Good and bad fortune being connected to good and bad acts. I have a feeling there is truth in this, even in Christian terms. If you are at a particular time somehow in touch with the good, with God, then – to use a picture word – the angels are around you and looking after you. You'll be alright.

There are a lot of books out now, by people like Richard Dawkins, that are rubbishing religion, telling us gleefully that God doesn't exist and only idiots believe in God. Those of us who believe in God can't prove it, they say. What they overlook is that they can't prove God doesn't exist. Stalemate? I'd say the believers have an advantage. Not that we can prove to anyone else that there is something more to life than just a job and a house and things to buy. But because we can prove *to ourselves* the reality of a divine dimension to our existence. We do it whenever we get in touch with it.

Isn't that what real prayer is about? And what meditation is about? Isn't it what sitting doing nothing, gazing into space, can be about? Leaning on a gate, maybe, looking at the earth and the sky. Or pausing for a moment when the Angelus bell rings. It's letting the God-ness of God into us, being in touch with God. Anyone can do it if they let themselves. You could almost say, if they pretend it's true and try it out, in the silence of their own heart. All books about God, even when they're pro-God, are only books. They are head-stuff, and it's not in the head but in the heart that we find God. The reality of our own personal experience is Reality with a capital R., the God of our experience. Ideas about God, doctrines and theology and teachings, all came out of experience. They are all the results of someone's experience. Some of them may be like our own, others not. Anything that anyone can say about God is always inadequate. As an anonymous writer said in the fourteenth century, 'By love God may be caught and held, by thinking never.'

I went to the beautiful Buddhist place on Beara last year, for a weekend retreat led by a Catholic priest. I knew the other people there would be a mixture of Christians and Buddhists, and thought it would be interesting to know how many there were of each. But it was an unanswerable question. So many were Catholics who also practise Buddhist meditation. Going to Mass one day, Dzogchen Beara the next day. There were three other Church of Ireland priests there, quite happy to be meditating with Buddhists. Some of us belong to Christian groups that practice meditation, or contemplative prayer. There are at least four such groups in West Cork, but the Churches don't seem to publicise them.

Maybe because they aren't part of the parish systems. In none of the four that I know would you be asked whether you are Catholic or Protestant, or any denomination at all. And that's part of their strength.

What that Buddhist retreat represented was the way so many people are looking for a deep experience of the divine, a sense that they don't seem to be getting from the institutional churches. In some churches, services are all made of words, as if they were entirely for the benefit of the brain, and not to touch the heart or the senses at all. Some others have been so keen, since the 1960s and '70s, to dump the God-in-the-sky idea, the God-out-there image, and replace it with God-is-among-us, that the congregation now sits in a circle and sings bouncy worship-songs together, and all the wonder and mystery has gone.

Deep down, straight out, what so many people want is God. A sense of the presence of God in their lives. Not a God they can know lots of things *about*, just a God they can *know*, within themselves. A God they can be in touch with. Not a God set apart for Sundays and special buildings but a God of the present moment, any moment, every moment. A God of the Now, found in sacred spaces and godly communities, but also wherever you are. Found in meditation, but also in a style of prayer so casual, so ordinary, that it is just chat. A God you can ask for what you want, for the sole reason that if it's important to you then it must also be important to this Source of your life that you are in touch with. A God that being in touch with somehow or other makes a difference, for you and for your world.

Of course we can't prove that at all, any more than we can prove the existence of love except by the effect it has. We don't have to try to prove it. All we have to do is to trust the heart.

4

This Christmas Celebrate and Give Thanks

The author wonders whether those who believe that Christmas is too religious are not left a little empty when it's all over and if they aren't nostalgic for that awe and wonder they once felt [22 December 2007]

It's nearly the time now. Nearly the time for all the expensive gifts, and the special foods, and the giddy, gaudy celebrations, the crowds, the parties, the laughter. Nearly the time, too, for all those memories of Christmases past, of the open-eyed wonder of childhood, the hush of church or chapel at midnight, the candles in the dark, and the lovely Christmas carols bursting out into the cold air, and going home among the stars to hot food and hugs and presents wrapped with love.

The numbers at midnight Mass and midnight services of Holy Communion are not what they were. Perhaps people find it too much trouble at such a busy time. Or it interferes with their own celebrations. Certainly many churches, in an attempt to avoid the embarrassments of drunken would-be participants, have moved midnight to a much earlier hour – and who wants to go to Midnight Mass at 8.00 pm?

Or there may be a more serious reason. Maybe it is too religious for some people. Maybe they look forward to all the fun of Christmas, and don't see why all that God-stuff should have anything to do with it, even if it did when they were young. But I wonder if they don't feel a little empty when it's all over and there's only the mess to clear up and the decorations to pull down. I wonder if they aren't somehow nostalgic for the awe and wonder they felt all those years ago, when going from the dark into the lit-up church or chapel was the beginning of the magical time. I wonder if they won't wish they had gone to the midnight service after all.

Those of us who try to keep some sort of overview of what is happening these days to Christianity are noticing a new trend. It's to do with that man from 2000 years ago. We call him Jesus, though he was probably called something like Joshua by his family and friends. A misty figure because so far back in time, yet intensely charismatic. It is this man who is surfacing out of the mess that we have made of Christianity, and suddenly being spot-lit. And it isn't 'The Church' – any church – that is doing it, but ordinary people.

'In a pub here,' someone said recently of a rather hippy town in England, 'you wouldn't choose to say you were a Christian. You'd probably get thrown out. But if you said you were a follower of Jesus – ah! – you'd probably be bought a drink.'

What seems to be happening is that fewer and fewer people are interested in all the traditional doctrines and creeds, and the divisions that those doctrines and creeds have brought. And what they are rediscovering of the Christian tradition is its central figure. That man who said that loving God and loving your neighbour were the main thing. That man who broke the rules of his own time and went and talked with people from other races and tribes, and with 'prostitutes and sinners', and with the tax-collectors who were loathed by everyone else. The man who thought healing people was a good thing to do even on the Sabbath. The man who told funny stories (we don't know they're funny because we are told them in such formal language). The man who didn't want to die, even though he must have recognised that it was the honesty of his own preachings and teachings that had made his execution inevitable.

This is the man who even lukewarm Christians are rediscovering. They're finding that his teachings about goodness and truth and love and peace and health and healing are enough to live by, whether you take them from the gospels of Matthew and Mark and Luke, or from the book of teachings called the 'Gospel of Thomas' which was written at about the same time but never made it into the Bible. Teachings like these:

'From Adam until John the Baptist, among the
    children begotten of women
there is none higher than John the Baptist. But I have
    said,

He who amongst you becomes as a child, shall know
    the Kingdom,
and shall be greater than John.'

'Let those who seek not cease from seeking until
    they find;
and when they find, they will be disturbed;
and when they are disturbed they will marvel,
and they shall reign over the All.'

'The kingdom of the Father is like a man who owned
    merchandise
and found a pearl. That merchant was wise:
he sold the merchandise, he bought this single pearl.
You also, seek after treasure which does not perish,
which no moth devours and no worm destroys.'

'If two make peace with each other
in this single house,
they will say to the mountain 'Move away'
and it shall move.'

How could the world not have a special day to commemorate
this brilliant man? We have no idea when he was born. Even
the year isn't known for sure, and certainly not the month
and day. But December 25 is as good a date as any other.
And even better than good, in this part of the world, when
you think about it being the time when the dark of the year
begins to turn towards the light. Because when life gets dark
and things begin to die down we all need to be reminded that

new life will come again. And that of course is what the Jesus story is all about. There will be death, but out of it will come life. Celebrating December 25 is saying that 2,000 years ago a man was born who grew up to be so good and so brave that he stuck to what he knew he was called by life to do, even though it meant his own death. A spirit like that lives on. A traditional Christian way of saying it is that the spirit of God was in that man, Jesus, and that that same spirit is with us still.

If you feel like going to church at Christmas time, go. Ignore what makes no sense to you, but join with the millions of others around the world who want to truly celebrate and give thanks for the birth of this amazing, once-only, man.

5

Christians Playing Their Part in Sustainability

The author has met many people who, through their
churches, are playing their part in the survival of creation
and who are helping to pull communities together to
work for the common good [19 January 2008]

Mention global warming and we're all capable of rushing to bury our heads in the sand. We might consider changing some light bulbs, and even getting more organised about recycling household waste. But if anyone is expecting us to go for a smaller car, or give up flying to the sunnier parts of the world for our holidays, we'd prefer not to think about it. If the little monkey in our brain is really clever, it will come up with all sorts of positive reasons for *not* doing anything about it. Like, the whole thing is nonsense, the weather's always been bit odd, people are just panicking. Or it's some sort of plot, by someone or other, and we're not going to fall into their trap.

Traditionally, Christianity is concerned about caring for God's creation. So you'd think we Christians would be out at the front when it comes to doing something about all the threats to the environment we are suddenly aware of. But not necessarily. 'I just trust in God,' one woman said, and presumably went on living in her old familiar creation-wasting way. ('Poor God,' some nuns said, when they heard that one.) A parish priest, who said the matter didn't inter-est him, was asked what would happen when the seas rise and sweep over Ireland. 'Ah, they can all go to America,' was his simple solution.

Church bells in Dublin and Clonakilty and other places rang out at 2.00 pm on December 2nd, at the initiative of the Stop Climate Chaos alliance. It was part of a general ap-peal to make a lot of noise at that time on that day, to draw attention to the world's climate problems. Supporting the appeal were groups like Christian Aid, Concern and Gorta, yet the only high-ranking church group to be included was the Methodist Church in Ireland's Council of Social Respon-sibility. A week before it happened, I asked a group of about a dozen local clergy here in West Cork if their church bells would be taking part. Only two of them knew anything about it.

Puzzling over all this, I went to see Jennifer Sleeman, of Clonakilty. Jennifer is the person mainly responsible for Clonakilty becoming the first Fair Trade town in Ireland. Last month she received an award from the Cork Environmental Forum in recognition of her 'outstanding contribution to sustainability in Cork city and county through partnership and participation in the promotion of environmental care'. She is also an active member of her local Catholic church.

'I am so disappointed in the clergy, and their attitude to the things that are going to afflict us all, like global warming,' she says. 'The clergy should be setting an example, and be seen to be doing it. There are exceptions, but most of them appear to be blind to it all.'

But if the church authorities are not involved, individual Christians certainly are. Most of Jennifer's energy is now going into the setting up of the new environmental group, Sustainability Clonakilty. She got involved because she found herself thinking about her grandchildren and wondering 'What are we doing to their world?' Then a friend from Newry came to see her. He had experienced the pulling together of the community there as, together, they faced up to the current threat to the environment.

Jennifer and a few others decided to show the film The End of Suburbia, in O'Donovan's hotel. Some locals were sceptical. 'You'll never get people to come and see that.' But they advertised it well, and filled the room twice. Al Gore's film was showing at the cinema in Clonakilty at about the

same time. Local people were roused. 'We must do more,'
they said. And so Sustainability Clonakilty was formed. Local
clergy Fr Gerard Galvin and the Revd Ian Jonas are suppor-
tive. It's been an informal group so far, but this month they
will have an AGM, elect a committee and make plans.

And some church congregations are stirring, thanks to a
new organisation called 'Eco-Congregation Ireland' that has
sprung up out of Churches Together in Britain and Ireland
(CTBI). Five churches are involved: the Roman Catholic
Church, the Church of Ireland, the Methodist Church in Ireland, the Presbyterian Church in Ireland and the Quakers.
Congregations are beginning to ask how many light bulbs are
on unnecessarily, and even whether they could install solar
panels on the church roof or geothermal heating under the
church floor. Parishes undertake an audit to work out how
environmentally sound they are. After that they get free access to resources to help them to integrate care for the environment into different areas of church life.

As soon as the Quakers in Cork heard about Eco-
Congregation Ireland they set up a public meeting called
'Caring for Creation'. Quaker Natasha Harty was impressed
with how many church people came to it. The Church of
Ireland bishop sent a representative, and there was an SMA
priest and a retired Columban priest. 'And *lots* of nuns,' she
says – 'they were great!' And there were many ordinary
churchgoers, of all denominations. The day was 'a resound-
ing success'. Since then there have been other events, including talks on the energy crisis, and on the ecological care
of graveyards, and a showing of the Al Gore film, *An Incon-
venient Truth*. Natasha Harty is full of information. 'If people

in West Cork are thinking they'd like to do something,' she says, 'they should get in touch with us. We can recommend any number of good speakers.'

One of those good speakers is the Revd John Purdy, of the Methodist circuit of West Cork. 'Eco-Congregation Ireland is designed to encourage everybody to greater ecological awareness,' he says. At first, some of the local farmers thought they were attacking the farming community, when they talked about Fair Trade produce. That is, until they realised the emphasis was also on locally produced food, organically grown, and animal-friendly.

What was Sustainability Clonakilty hoping for, I asked Jennifer Sleeman. 'We would like to see us all reducing our carbon footprint, especially the town council but also individuals and businesses. Changing our lifestyles is very important now, or we are heading for disaster. People say, 'What difference can *I* make?' but if everybody makes changes we can make a huge difference. We want to get the hearts and minds of people.'

Another way to go is that of the Transition Towns. Kinsale is the first such town in all of Ireland. According to the TT website, 'A Transition Initiative is a community that is unleashing its own latent collective genius to look Peak Oil and Climate Change squarely in the eye and to discover and implement ways to address this big question.'

So there is no shortage of ways for churches to get involved in the survival of creation. If the people of Newry are any indication, groups like Sustainability are good in two ways. Not only do they work for the good of the planet and the future life of our grandchildren, but they also pull com-

munities together, across denominational or sectarian di-
vides, and political differences. How could that *not* be an essential part of the work of our churches?

(For more information, see www.sustainabilityclonakilty.com,
www.eco-congregationireland.org and www.transitiontowns.org)

6

Only We Can Decide Where Our Future Lies

The author has a look into her crystal ball and sees two
distinctly divergent paths that Christianity may follow.
Which way will things go? The choice is ours.
[2 February 2008]

I'm looking into the future. In my crystal ball, which is a
gathering together of all that I know about the churches,
especially in this country, the clouds are shifting, and I can see
– nothing. The churches are all gone, the church buildings
derelict or turned into shops and houses. Christianity is dead,
killed by the frenzied love of getting and spending that came
with an economic growth too rapid for us to cope with. People are locked into their own houses and apartments, in
smaller and smaller family groups. Community is dead.

But wait, that picture is fading and the clouds are shifting again. An alternative image is coming up. There are churches but they look different. Beautiful, colourful buildings, full of life. People pouring in and out, women and men, babies and children. Stopping to talk, to play, to help. We're going inside the building now, and here too it is full of colour, and music, and light, all to delight the senses and lift the heart. A group of musicians are practising, and around them are ancient and modern works of art. In a side room the light is dimmed, there are candles and stillness, a space for people to be with God in quietness.

But where are the priests, the ministers, the clergy? There is no-one in black with a white collar. No one walking about looking as if they own the place. Someone explains it all to us. The clergy are part of the team. They are not paid, but have a normal job like everyone else. They have been chosen by the community for their capacity to inspire goodness and godliness, their ability to encourage spiritual growth. They lead part of the regular worship and speak words of wisdom to the community. But they have no responsibility for the upkeep of the building, or fund-raising, or any other sort of administration, or the social work groups. All those things, including pastoral care of the community, are done by others with the relevant skills and knowledge. These are also unpaid, except that in the larger urban parishes sometimes a salaried administrator is hired by the community. In the past it was found that having one person as the spiritual 'big boss' was unhealthy for the congregation, which was infantilised – 'Daddy will do it'. It was also unhealthy for the leader himself (and in the old days it was usually a man). Too much was expected of that one person, and what he did was generally not valued because he was paid to do it. And because such leaders were perceived as different they were isolated from the normal friendship of the community. In some cases they were not allowed to marry, thus increasing their isolation and loneliness.

Changes started to happen when the number of clergy began to drop seriously. From the 1970s onwards people had started to drift away from the churches, partly because their own views were ignored and partly because there were ever more interesting things to do. In the Roman Catholic Church, fewer and fewer men wanted to become priests. By 2007, of just over 3,000 diocesan priests in Ireland, a quarter were retired. Half were over 60, and there were only 24 new seminarians that year. So, parish councils and steering groups were introduced, involving men and women. As the laity found its voice, the demand for married priests and women priests became undeniable. 'Prayers for vocations', urged by the church hierarchy, were answered by men and women of every sort.

Meanwhile the Church of Ireland, whose numbers going into ministry had remained fairly steady, was facing the financial problems common to all the churches. But it also was concerned about clergy. In 2007 a Bishops' Planning Group was set up to look at ministry in twenty-first century Ireland. The Bishop of Clogher said: 'The role of the rector has undergone a thorough transformation in the last 30 years. In order to prepare people effectively ... a radical rethink of our approach to preparation for ministry is required.' How radical? It was to involve 'a close bond be-

tween study and practice ... lifelong learning, deepening vocation, spiritual self-awareness and integrity of living.' It
didn't sound very radical. And indeed, it was all to do with
the training of full-time clergy and the future of the Church
of Ireland's theological college.

In the end, God moved in mysterious ways, and finances
dictated change. As congregations shrank, and fewer and
fewer people were asked to raise more and more money,
something snapped. The bishops' 'radical rethink' turned
into something much bigger than re-arranging the deck-
chairs. Clergy started to work for nothing, and found a new
sense of freedom and joy. Congregations started to pull together and to grow, as they took on pastoral and administrative responsibilities with a new creative energy. Education
and training were available for all, not just for clergy. Worship came alive, and with it a new commitment to each
other and to the protection of all of creation.

And now in the crystal ball I see other new things happening, things begun from the grassroots. People are going
into churches wherever they like, wherever they find spiritual food and inspiration. The old idea that they should not
receive communion in 'other' churches has been dropped,
after they began to ask whether Jesus ever turned people
away from his table. Doctrinal issues have simply been sidelined by those for whom they made no sense, although others remain happy with them. Liturgy is everywhere varied,
being beautifully solemn in some places, Quakerly quiet and
meditative in others, lively and joyful in others. Religion is
taught in schools only as an academic subject, but children
become part of the religious community by full participation

in it from the earliest age. Methodists and Presbyterians, after a time of shrinkage and church closures, have become in many ways the social conscience of Irish Christianity, leading the way in concern for problems at home and in the wider world. Ecumenism, which at one time was seen as demanding 'a single voice' for Christianity, has taken wings with the new vision of acknowledging and accepting diversity – 'creating a space in which we can listen to our differences and the giftedness of the other tradition,' as the general secretary of Churches Together in Britain and Ireland said in January 2008. A wonderful vision.

But now I am putting down the crystal ball. It can't really decide which way things will go. Only we can do that.

7

West Cork People Feel Blessed to Work in 'Daddy Home'

The author on the work done at the home for children in India run by Fr Raja Reddy [16 February 2008]

'I feel so blessed to be part of it,' Irene Dowd says, as we talk about the children's home in India where Fr Raja Reddy and others care for hundreds of young ones, orphaned or destitute. Irene is one of the team-leaders at the Fr Raja Charity Shop in Schull, which raises money for the

home. She has been to India twice as a volunteer assistant
with the children. Recently in Schull an amateur film of the
home was shown by two other local women who have just
returned from volunteer work there.

Rosemarie Isenschmid had been there three years earlier, when the home was very new, and she was amazed at
the improvements. 'Three years ago it was bare desert
ground. The children sat on the sand. Now there are trees
and fruit and vegetable gardens, melons and courgettes and
spinach and chillis, nuts and herbs. All growing on soil
brought up load by load from the river. Everyone helps, including the children. Now they are all fed with organic fruit
and vegetables.'

It is known as the 'Daddy Home', because those are
both words the children can understand. And it does seem
like a real home. The children help with the gardening and
the housework before they go to school. 'Everywhere is so
clean,' Rosemarie says. But there is also time for playing. In
the film we saw the children dancing, and playing a huge en-
thusiastic game of Blind Man's Buff in the courtyard with Fr
Raja. Some were playing cricket, others were absorbed in a
game of chess.

Agnes Goyvaert from Skibbereen went with Rosemarie
to work at the home. She was impressed with the care
taken of the many children who come there HIV positive, or
even having AIDS, often from birth. They receive extra food
to complement their medication, and they have monthly
hospital appointments to monitor their condition. Some
have been found abandoned, others brought in by the surviving but dying parent and the home cares for them both.

One baby, adopted by an Indian couple, had been thrown in a bin when they discovered he had AIDS.

The small farm at the home, with buffaloes and cows, is managed by a young woman who was bought out of slavery by Fr Raja, and now has her own family. Fr Raja's mother cares for the street children in a nearby town. The gardens at the home are under the care of his disabled father, a Grandfather to the children. But there is no shortage of grandparents. A number of destitute elderly people have been taken in, and there is a real connection between the younger children and the elderly. And between the children themselves. New ones are readily accepted by the others, and soon part of a happy group. 'The older children care for the younger ones,' Agnes says. 'It seems to come naturally.'

Schooling is considered vitally important. Teachers at the village school, about a mile away, are government supported. For older children there is vocational training at the home for mechanical work, carpentry and plumbing, social work, driving tuition, sewing and embroidery, computers, crafts. But Fr Raja is hoping to create a second-level school in the town, where his children can mix with children from ordinary families. In the film seen in Schull he talks about his hopes for the children. He has a passionate concern for the dignity of each of them. The gap between the haves and the have-nots is so large, he says, and he wants them to learn to be self-sufficient.

Agnes was especially impressed by the meeting of the whole 'family', that takes place every month. Every person, child or adult, is asked by Fr Raja if there are any problems.

'And he is very good at drawing them out!' Each one gets his or her say, and suggestions are given.

In front of the home there is a large swimming pool, which is also used for watering the vegetable gardens. There are solar panels providing electricity, and a transformer. According to Rosemary, 'Fr Raja is always thinking ahead.' As well as the senior school, he is planning a dispensary (especially needed for the HIV/AIDS children), and a home of their own for the elderly.

All this, from land that a few years ago was dry and bare, is wonderful. While Agnes and Rosemarie were there Fr Raja received two awards on behalf of the home. The first was in recognition of 'one of the 40 best homes for AIDS patients' in India. The other was as the 'Charity of the Year' of the state of Andhra Pradesh – which is about the size of Ireland. The home has the full support of the local Catholic bishop and diocese, and the Bon Secours Sisters provide three much-loved nuns who look after the day-to-day needs of the children. When small children come into the home it is often not known what their faith background is, and all faiths are provided for. The logo for the home is called 'A Symbol of Religious Unity: Hindu, Muslim, Christian' and shows the three faith symbols intertwined.

One of the most basic needs is for volunteers. Most of those who have been are keen to return as soon as possible. Volunteers can choose their work, from feeding the smaller children, and mending clothes and toys, to garden and farm work. There are young volunteers, from Germany and Austria in particular, but Fr Raja would like to have more of all ages from Ireland. English is the common language in India, and it will improve the children's future employment opportunities if their English is fluent. Even the girls who teach the children would benefit from tuition, as their grasp of the language is not always very good.

The other basic need is for sponsorship, providing funds to run the home and build the dispensary and the second-level school, and increase the farm stock of cows and buffaloes. Two hundred of the children have sponsors, but more are needed. The money sent is shared among all, but sponsored children have a special relationship with their sponsors, and are helped to write letters to them from time to time. The person to contact about this, through the charity shop in Main Street, Schull, is Elizabeth Hicks. She visited the Daddy Home when it opened in 2005, and says 'We are greatly privileged to be involved in such an extraordinary enterprise.'

At the Schull shop the staff members are all local volunteers, a great mix of different nationalities and faiths. All the shop profits go to the Home. So everyone who comes in to give or buy there is also involved in this 'extraordinary enterprise'.

'We build so many temples,' Fr Raja says. 'This is a great temple of humanity – help us to build it.'

8

The God-experience Has Escaped Out of the Box

The author tells us that sitting in an alert but relaxed
silence with others can be a deeply spiritual experience,
strengthening and enlarging [1 March 2008]

The phrase 'the sacrament of the present moment' was created almost 300 years ago, by a shy French priest called Jean-Pierre de Caussade. Yet suddenly it seems to be right in the centre of twenty-first century spirituality. The modern writer Eckhardt Tolle has rushed into the best-seller lists with his books on the importance of the 'Now'. More and more writers and spiritual leaders are echoing de Caussade's message that the divine is present in every moment of our lives. 'God makes of *all* things mysteries and sacraments of love. Why should not every moment of our lives be a sort of communion with the divine?'

The idea that you can 'experience the divine' is something that has escaped out of the closed communities of the churches and is out there in the streets now, for everyone. Maybe this has happened because the churches didn't value it enough. Modernisation of worship has had a lot going for it, and has done much good, but a price has been paid for it. We have lost silence and mystery, and awe and wonder, from our Eucharists and services. And it isn't that we haven't noticed. In the last decade or so, a surprising number of Irish Christians have become Quakers. At a time when there is a general bemoaning that church numbers would be going right down if it wasn't for the immigrants, Quaker numbers are going up. It's fairly safe to say that the main attraction is silence. A Quaker meeting is usually an hour or so of sitting in silence. People may stand and speak briefly if they feel inspired to do so, but then the silence takes over again.

Other Christians now combine Buddhist meditation with their Christianity. Again, it is the silence that is the draw. Many of them are probably practising a form of meditation that is more Christian than Buddhist, but no one minds. Just to sit in an alert but relaxed silence with others can be a deeply spiritual experience, strengthening and enlarging. It's something that we don't generally find in our own churches.

The sad thing is that this practice of silence was part of Christianity from the beginning, and then was just about lost in the sixteenth century. For political-theological reasons, of course. Some held on to it. People like St Teresa of Avila, George Herbert, St John of the Cross, and numbers of long-forgotten, never-known, men and women in Catholic and Protestant contemplative orders. In the twentieth century it was rediscovered by lay people and they began to meet together, in houses or chapels or churches or parish halls. They called what they were doing contemplative prayer or, using a more modern term, Christian meditation. Groups and organisations came into being across the world to promote the experience. There is the World Community of Christian Meditation (WCCM), which is basically Roman Catholic, and the Fellowship of Contemplative Prayer (FCP), which is basically Anglican (Church of Ireland/England etc.) and – the one I know best – the Julian Meetings (JM), which has been ecumenical from the start. JM is also the least structured, encouraging people to find by experiment their own best way into silence, rather than promoting a particular method. (www.julianmeetings.org)

What do people do when they meditate? In a way, the word is misleading, because you don't meditate *on* anything, or think *about* anything. The opposite, really. You let the thinking part of your head switch off, or drift off. The word 'contemplation' is a bit better. You contemplate what is. What you hope to experience is 'the sacrament of the present moment'. To be totally present in the Now – which is not easy. Perhaps you let your senses guide you, becoming aware of what you can see, hear, smell, feel, taste. So that the past and the future fall away and what is, in this moment, is all that is. If the word 'God' has meaning for you, then contemplating what is includes contemplating the God that is everywhere about you, without and within. Not thinking *about* God – no doctrines, no pictures in your head – but simply allowing yourself to experience the 'is-ness' of God.

Some retreat houses, like Myross Wood near Skibbereen, offer teaching in contemplation, with regular gatherings. And some of the above groups go for their own sessions to local retreat houses, or convents or monasteries, because there they can find spaces of calm quietness.

Some of our churches have recognised this growing desire for silence and awe in worship, and responded to it. Taizé, the ecumenical community in France where hundreds of people, mainly young, gather from all over the world for a week or more at a time, has been very influential. Its worship sessions and its Eucharists, held in huge marquees, are candle-lit and quiet, with the singing of songs that are soft and short and repetitive, often leading naturally into periods of silence. In Ireland and other countries now, some churches are providing Taizé-style worship.

As a nation, despite the present childish materialism we will soon – please God – outgrow, we are becoming more aware of the place that spirituality plays in our lives. We are learning to value sacred spaces and 'thin places' wherever we find them. We are discovering spiritual experiences in art and music and film and drama. The divine, which we thought was boxed up in dreary old churches, has escaped out of the box into our daily lives. Our churches still have a place, and it could indeed be a very valuable place. What they do not have is a monopoly. They don't own God. But they *are* communities where we can come together to share our experience of God, and all that grows in love and integrity out of that.

9

Keeping the Traditions but Allowing the Changes

The author gives some examples where, as in most religions, there is always a conflict between tradition and change [15 March 2008]

We used to spell it 'Koran'; now it's the Qur'an. It's the holy book of Islam, the eternal word of God, revealed by the angel Gabriel to the prophet Muhammad (570–632 CE). It began when the angel came to him on Mount Hira, near Mecca, and gave him words to recite. Muhammad, who was about 40 years of age, could not read or write, but his wife Khadija encouraged him, and he dictated all the words that were gradually given to him. The resulting Qur'an is about the size of the New Testament of Christianity. Its core message is that there is only one God; that good or bad lives result in rewards or punishments after death; that business must be done with honesty, and that there should be concern for the poor.

Associated with the Qur'an is the Hadith, narrations of the life of the prophet and his companions. Sometimes described as a clarification of the Qur'an, it is a guide to the behaviour expected of Muslims and influences sharia, the Islamic law.

Last month sharia was in the news, after the Archbishop of Canterbury, the head of the Anglican church, asked the legal establishment in Britain whether certain aspects of Islamic law could and should be made available, by choice, under the law of the UK for 'resolving disputes and regulating transactions'. This was of course only relating to civil law. Unfortunately, large sections of the media and the public heard this as suggesting that harsh public punishments for theft or adultery could become part of British legal system. Not so.

And last week the Hadith was in the news, after it was announced that Turkey's department of religious affairs has begun a major revision of it. That news has given hope to many that it will produce a twenty-first century form of Islam, resulting in an end to discrimination against women, and the banishing of some of those severe penalties of old, such as stoning and amputation. One Turkish commentator has said that the work is nearly finished, but that there are difficulties where the writings concern the treatment of women. One solution, he says, would be to delete them altogether, as not being authentic but having been added a couple of hundred years after the death of Muhammad. Another would be to add footnotes, declaring that they should be understood simply as the product of a different age.

It has often been said that, unlike the Anglican and Protestant churches, Islam has never been through a Reformation. This revision is possibly the beginning of such a Reformation. On the other hand, some scholars say it is merely a return to the original Islam, the faith that existed before layers of writings and laws were laid onto it.

Certainly such a Reformation would have a tremendous effect on the world's image of Islam. Too often Muslims are seen as nothing but fundamentalists with brutish ideas of justice and dreams of terrorism. Yet this is a caricature of basic Islam, which is a devout and godly religion with much in common with Christianity and Judaism.

This revision of the Hadith has an interesting reflection in Christianity. Aren't there a great many aspects of Christian faith that were 'add-ons' to the original, and which are now causing problems? We can think of things like the requirement of celibacy for Catholic priests, which certainly wasn't asked by Jesus of his followers. Most of them, unless very young, would have been married. The First Letter of Paul to Timothy, in the New Testament, says that a bishop should be 'above reproach, and married only once'. The ban on marriage for the clergy was only brought in much later. In some parts of the church it came in during the fourth century, but in other parts not until the eleventh century. And even then it was resisted for a time. Increasing numbers in the Catholic Church think it should go now, and it is not hard to imagine what huge changes that would make for Catholics all over the world.

And we can think of things like the '39 Articles', which are a part of the worldwide Anglican Church including the Church of Ireland. These 'Articles of Religion', as they were called in the pre-1984 Prayer Book, were written in the sixteenth century, a time of terrible conflict in England between Catholics and Protestants. They include statements such as 'the Church of Rome hath erred, not only in [its] living and manner of ceremonies, but also in matters of Faith' (Article

19). They are nasty about what they call 'Romish' ideas of purgatory, pardons and praying to the saints (Article 22). Their lack of relation to the modern world is capped by the requirement that 'General Councils may not be gathered together without the commandment and will of Princes'. All of these may be understandable when viewed in the light of what was happening in the world in the sixteenth century. Yet these Articles of the Church of England were 'received and approved by the Archbishops and bishops and the rest of the clergy of Ireland' in the seventeenth century and by all of them again, plus the laity, in the nineteenth century. In some countries the Anglican Church has distanced itself from them. Not yet so in Ireland, sadly. The best we can say is that at least they weren't included in the 'Alternative' Prayer Book which the Church of Ireland brought out in 1984. But, shockingly, the original set of Articles was then included in the new Book of Common Prayer published by the Church in 2004. So the document is still there, still in existence, still being circulated as part of the 'historic formularies' of the Church. That surely is another 'add-on' which should now be taken off.

In all the great religions of the world there is always a conflict between tradition and change. To throw out all tradition is like chopping up your life-raft in a heaving sea. But to change nothing is like piling more and more furniture and possessions onto the raft so that it eventually submerges. Either way, you drown. St Teresa's prayer is a good one: 'God, give me the courage to change what needs changing, the strength to accept what cannot be changed, and the wisdom to know the difference.'

10

Kindness and Liberality

An Ireland of neighbours [29 March 2008]

Something really sad is happening to us, here in Ireland. We ought to be happy, with our increased ability to buy all the things that make life enjoyable. But we're not happy, as the increasing use of drink and drugs shows. Now, it seems, we are the worst country in Europe for binge-drinking. The rising incidence of road rage reflects our un-happiness, and the mounting number of tragic road accidents is the result.

Then there is the suicide rate. Some years ago it started to rocket up among young men. Often they were farmers, leading fairly isolated lives. And we were shocked, of course. Now there is a new concern. Here in the affluent paradise of West Cork young mothers are joining the ranks of the suicides. They leave children, husbands, families and neighbours devastated. Why they would do it is a question we can ask, but can probably only ever guess at answers.

Part of it may be that our growing consumerism seems to drive out neighbourliness. Someone said on RTE Radio 1 recently that foreign tourists coming to Ireland for the first time would not find the Ireland they were expecting if they arrived first into Dublin. They'd have to go out to the West, the speaker said, to experience the 'Bord Fáilte Ireland'. The implication was that the Ireland of the old days still exists in rural areas. That there you will still find the slow pace of life, the warmth of welcome, and the neighbourliness that the cities have lost. And surely to some extent that is true. Here in West Cork, for example, most of us are cocooned by being part of a community. People who know each other, who stop to talk to each other on the streets of our towns and villages. People who look after their neighbours when help is needed or illness strikes.

Yet maybe it won't be like this for ever, and maybe the change is already creeping in. Even here we spend more time alone with our possessions, and do less things together than we used to. Here, as in the rest of Ireland, it is increasingly difficult to get people out of their homes to go to meetings or events. Adults and children, we are withdrawing into our own four walls. Children who in the past would have wandered outdoors with other children, playing and exploring and creating a world of imagination, now sit indoors at their incredibly expensive PlayStations. We own more and more of the computers and phones and iPods that seduce us into immersing ourselves in technological isolation. We have fewer meals with other people, preferring the easy snack food that doesn't take us out of our solo-bubble.

We don't actually *need* each other – or so it seems.

What we seem to think we need is more and more things. More stuff. Relationships are just trouble, so we'll buy a bigger better television, and a Rolex watch, and a larger house. Then we'll really be, at last, as happy as all the advertisements promise. But we're not.

Are we on the wrong track altogether? When this country emerged out of centuries of grey poverty and oppression where – the only light came from going to church – into the suddenness of a multi-coloured Tiger economy – where dazzling light pours out from a million shops – did it go a bit mad? Is it maybe all just a phase, an understandable response to that enormous change?

Materialism, an urge to acquire possessions, is a common reaction to the insecurity brought on by sudden change. On their holidays, people tend to buy things they would not buy in their normal daily life. When they get home they wonder what possessed them to have bought such a thing. If they stay in that holiday location long enough to feel secure, their interests turn to non-material things like the landscape, or the music or history of the place, or the people.

The word 'wealth' originally meant 'well-being'. The strength of community is the real well-being of us all. So how do we as a nation make the move from obsession with the false wealth of consumerism to re-building or safeguarding community?

The Vatican has suggested – not just to Ireland but to the world – that the old word 'sin' is still valid. It has produced an update to the Seven Deadly Sins. As well as the original Seven, which are mostly the failings of individuals (pride, covetousness, lust, anger, gluttony, envy, sloth), we should be aware, it says, of the sins of our new age such as drug abuse, and environmental pollution, and – yes – 'accumulating excessive wealth'. And we should avoid causing poverty, and creating social inequalities and social injustice. We probably think we don't personally create such effects. But you could argue that by allowing our governments to perpetrate them we are at the very least colluding with them.

Unfortunately, the Vatican didn't provide an update on the Seven Heavenly Virtues. Sometimes we react better to being shown a vision of the Good than to being berated for our badness. There are two versions of that list of virtues. The more traditional is: faith, hope, charity, fortitude. justice, prudence and temperance. Not at all a bad recipe for a good world, if you think about them. Another version is a list of antidotes to the Seven Deadly Sins. So against pride you get humility, against envy there is kindness, in place of gluttony there is abstinence and so on, producing chastity, patience, liberality and diligence. Some of those words we're very un-comfortable with ('abstinence', chastity'), but they can use-fully be re-worked. Others are capable of changing us utterly with one word. 'Kindness' alone could almost create a para-dise. And 'liberality' instead of greed is a beautiful ideal.

Will we get there? Can Ireland again be a land of saints and neighbours? Yes, if enough of us want it. And say so. And do something about it, individually and collectively.

11

Three Men in a Church –
But What about the Women?

*The author wonders if it would be better for all of us if
the word 'God' was seen to include maleness and
femaleness? [12 April 2008]*

'Father, Son and Holy Spirit', we Christians traditionally
say when we are talking about the three ways of God
being God. The Trinity. But most of us aren't really thinking
of them as three ways of being. We are thinking of them as
three men. The first one with a long white beard, the second one with a short brown beard, and the third one – well,
that's difficult. The third one doesn't really have a face, and
is a sort of ghost, or sometimes a dove, but definitely male.

Some church people choose to replace those words
with the genderless phrase 'Creator, Redeemer and Sus-
tainer' or 'Creator, Redeemer and Sanctifier'. I have known
people use it in my own Anglican church for the past twenty
years or so. It must be happening in the Roman Catholicism
too, because the Pope has now spoken against it, saying that
if such a phrase is used in baptism the sacrament is not valid.

It's obvious that how we think of God affects not only
how we pray but all of our religious faith. It also affects our
view of ourselves. The Christian church has such a long tradition of putting women down, almost from the beginning.

Going right against the attitude of Jesus, who counted
women as his friends, Tertullian (c.160-230) called them 'the
devil's gateway'. St Augustine (354-430) said that woman
was not in the image of God unless she was with a man.
Others denied that women had souls. Even if we ignore
these ancient sentiments we're still left with hundreds of
years of prayers and hymns in which we all called ourselves
'sons of God', 'men of God', and spoke in the Creed of 'us
men and our salvation'. All of these seemed to suggest that
the male version of humanity is the norm, and that the female is some sort of unimportant minority. That tradition
has done a huge amount of damage – to women and to men
– and therefore to the health of the whole church. It is
gradually being changed. But some church authorities resist
the change. (Interestingly, so do some women.)

What effect does all this male language have, I wonder,
on Christian women? Do we heterosexual women, in the
depths of our hearts, enjoy having an all-male God? Is that
why there are usually more women in church than men?
And what does it do for Christian men? How different
would Christianity be for men if God were all-female? More
seriously, would it be better for all of us if the word 'God'
was seen to include maleness and femaleness?

It isn't only since the rise of feminism that God has been
given female attributes. Back in the fourteenth century the
hermit Julian of Norwich was saying, 'As truly as God is our
Father, so truly also God is our Mother.' Praying to 'God our
Mother' feels strange, but logically it shouldn't, because God is
not a human being at all, and is therefore no more male than

female. In fact, praying to God as Mother can be helpful for those who have had problems with their real-life fathers.

People of other faiths sometimes think that Mary the mother of Jesus is the female aspect of the Christian God, but this is always denied. All the same, the veneration and affection that is shown for Mary by Roman Catholics and by some 'high' Anglicans, and the prayers that are offered to her, do go some way towards feminising the divine. For 'low' Anglicans, and for the Protestant churches such as the Presbyterian and Methodist, there is no such feminine aspect. Wouldn't it save it all if the genderless Holy Spirit was called 'she'? Indeed, the word 'spirit' was female once. The Book of Genesis, shared by Jews and Christians, begins by describing the creation of the heavens and the earth. It says, 'God's spirit hovered over the water'. The Hebrew word for 'spirit' is *Ruach,* and is female. You'd have to wonder why Christianity turned it into a male word. You could also wonder what harm it would do if we reclaimed it as a female word.

It's sad that our religious education rarely extends beyond our school days, so we carry childish ideas into our adult lives. Many people imagine God as a man because when they talk of God they really mean the man Jesus. A letter in one of our national newspapers a while back said, 'God actually is a human being, and one quite critical of religious institutions.' I suspect the writer was referring to Jesus. A ten-year old once told me, 'I pray to Jesus, but when I'm grown up I'll pray to God.' It takes some sort of maturity to go beyond the human image of Jesus into a sense of God as a divine spirit that fills all of creation and is greater than all of creation. 'The ground of our being,' was how the theologian Paul Tillich described God, and that description works for many of us.

If the Trinity, those three ways of God being God, in-cludes the Creator God (neither male nor female but encom-passing both) and the man Jesus (male) and the Spirit of God (female), there is a beautiful balance. In the early days of women priests in Anglican churches such as the Church of Ireland, the Church of England and the Episcopal Church of the USA, many people were still against the ordination of women. Yet a lot of them were converted to it when they experienced the ministry of men and women standing at the altar together. What got through to them, they said, was that they saw with their own eyes that male and female comple-mented each other and made for wholeness. So that the con-gregations felt that they had been balanced and made whole, too. That day has not yet come for Roman Catholics, nor for some Presbyterian congregations in this island. Maleness and femaleness, in God and in ourselves. It will surely come soon.

12

'Empowering the World's Poorest Communities'

The author tells us about her meeting with Ramila
Leathard, who has worked for Christian Aid for 20 years
[26 April 2008]

'I'm glad to be doing the work I'm doing. It's my way of putting my faith into action, but it makes me feel a bit guilty sometimes, going back to the safety of my own home,' says Ramila Leathard. Born in Sri Lanka, and now living with her priest-husband in London, Ramila has worked for Christian Aid for 20 years and is currently the Programme Manager for Burma. She was in Ireland recently to talk to groups in Cork, Belfast and Dublin.

When we met in Bandon, we talked mostly about Burma. Like Tibet, the country is in the news this year because Buddhist monks have been protesting about the way their country is governed. Burma has huge problems, not least with malaria, TB, and HIV/AIDS. The HIV rate is the second highest in south-east Asia. Initially it was spread by the use of drugs, but now more and more by sexual activity, mainly heterosexual. In some other countries with high incidence of HIV the drugs needed to combat the disease are given free by the government. It doesn't happen in Burma.

'The Ministry of Health is beginning to work on the problem,' Ramila says. 'But they need to be more organised. Christian Aid works through local organisations in Burma, and we are encouraging church leaders to counteract the prejudice which exists against people with HIV.'

Many Burmese people have fled their home country, going over the borders into China and Thailand. There some merge into the general population, and are 'lost'. But most of them register with the office of the United Nations High Commissioner for Refugees (UNHCR) and settle into refugee camps just over the border.

'The camps are run by the refugees themselves,' Ramila says. 'Christian Aid aims to train them up in work that will benefit them later. They grow vegetables, learn about nutrition. One man, a former engineer, has perfected organic farming techniques, and a manual based on his work has been produced, for other camps.'

'Many refugees are hoping to return to their homeland. But some have been in camps for 25 years. Some of course re-settle in other countries. But that is not ideal, as they tend to be the people with the special skills, like teaching and medicine. So those skills are creamed off.'

To give a picture of life in the refugee camps, Ramila spoke about Mwookwer. His name means 'living man'. Yet he feels he is only 'half a man'. His village was destroyed and in escaping he stepped on a landmine and lost a leg. He came to the camps in the late 1980s, with his wife, and they now have two children. He is a Christian, as are four per cent of the population of Burma. Formerly a maths teacher, he now teaches in the camp. The dream of returning to Burma one

day, Ramila says, is what 'keeps him believing, facing the future, sustains him'.

'These are wonderful people,' she says. But the conditions in which they exist make her feel 'a bit guilty sometimes, going back to the safety of my own home'. She adds,
'Burma is a beautiful country, with a huge thirst for education. Christian Aid's motto is "Life before death". It's all
about dignity, and human rights, and empowering people.
We are trying to build community by strengthening the
voice of the people.'

Mrs Leathard's activities are in three areas. She works
with refugees in the camps just outside Burma. She also
works inside Burma, mostly with local organisations. These
would be of all denominations, through the Council of
Churches, and all faiths, since a huge majority of the people
are Buddhists. And she works in the London office, dissemi-
nating information, providing training for smaller groups,
supporting organisations like the Asian Human Rights Commission, and pressuring the UK government to increase aid
to Burma. (It hadn't escaped her attention that Ireland's per
capita rate of aid to the developing world is almost twice
that of the UK.)

She sums up her work as, 'Telling the story, alleviating
poverty, challenging the structures.'

In all of this she is supported by Christian Aid Ireland,
the official relief and development agency of the Irish Council of Churches. Member churches of the Council are the
Church of Ireland, the Presbyterian Church in Ireland, the
Non-subscribing Presbyterian Church in Ireland, the Methodist Church in Ireland, the Moravian Church, the Religious

Society of Friends (Quakers), and the Salvation Army. The churches work together, with communities and with individuals, across denominations and religions.

During her visit to Ireland Ramila Leathard was the keynote speaker at a conference held at the Methodist Church at the Ardfallen Centre in Cork. The theme of the conference was 'Empowering the World's Poorest Communities' and centered specifically on the work of Christian Aid and its partners in Burma. Mrs Leathard provided a unique insight of the work of Christian Aid partners within the confines of the political and social environment of that country.

As a result of that meeting, a Cork Christian Aid Supporters' Committee has been formed. It has representatives of a number of church communities within the city and from the county. First among the committee's activities will be the organisation of events during Christian Aid Week, which this year is from May 11 to 17. Supporters and volunteers in Cork – and throughout Ireland, of course – will be helping in the organisation of coffee parties and other fund-raising events to support the work of the charity and its partners in the developing world. Andrew Coleman is the Co-ordinator for South West Ireland, based in Bandon. He says the week will be 'seven amazing days of fundraising, prayer, and action against world poverty.' Resource packs for coffee parties are available, with leaflets, posters, coffee sachets, and balloons. Andrew can be contacted at cork@christian-aid.org, or by phone at 023 41468.

13

The Power of Living in the Present Moment

The author believes that living in the present moment,
rather than in the past or in the future, can be incredibly
good for us [10 May 2008]

'Living in the present moment' sounds like something we all do without even thinking about it. But few of us do it. Some of the time we are back in the past, re-living events, maybe of the distant past, maybe of something that happened yesterday or an hour ago. And getting annoyed about it, or upset, or happy or nostalgic or sad. Some of the time we're off into the future with worries and anxieties, or hopes and dreams. That leaves just a fraction of time when we are living in the present moment. It's usually when we're doing something practical that takes all our attention, like mending something or drawing a picture.

Small children mostly live in the present. It's only as they get older that the past and the future lay hold on them. Watch a young child watching a caterpillar or an ant. They are so into it that they are unaware of anything else. It's total concentration. Any sort of child's-play takes place in the 'now'. That 'now'-ness, that ability to be in the present, is something we adults have almost lost. And yet it is incredibly good for us.

There's a book called *The Power of Now* by Eckhart Tolle that has been way up on the best-seller lists for quite a while now. It's a lot like religion, and quotes Jesus sometimes, but it appeals just as much and perhaps more to those who have dumped religion. Because it tells us that by living more and more in the present moment we can free ourselves from the hurt of the past and fear of the future. It tells us how we can get out of pain, find peace, and be transformed into a new and very alive person.

The idea of the importance of living in the 'now' is not new. There's a whole history of this practice hidden in Christianity, for a start. There was Meister Eckhart, born in Germany in the year 1260. (Tolle has been so influenced by him that he named himself after him.) Meister Eckhart, like Jesus, says that the Kingdom of God is within you. So you don't have to go looking for it, only let go, be still, and allow it surface. 'God is born in us as soon as all our soul-powers, which until now have been tied and bound, are absolutely free,' he says. And freedom comes when the mind and the senses are still.

Centuries after Eckhart came Brother Lawrence, and his beautiful little book *The Practice of the Presence of God*. Born in France around 1614, he had been a soldier, then a hermit, then a footman, and finally entered a Carmelite priory as a lay brother. His book is another joyful assertion of the good that comes from living in the Now. Sent to work in the priory kitchens, he was happy, putting himself consciously in the presence of God while he laboured. 'I am as much at prayer in the kitchen,' he wrote, 'as when I am on my knees before the Blessed Sacrament.' So he too was an advocate of living in the Now, as an awareness of the presence of God is only available in the present moment.

Half a century later there was Jean-Pierre de Caussade, another Frenchman, another advocate of living in the present. His writings are translated under various titles, like *Abandonment to Divine Providence*, but the one that seems most attractive in this century is *The Sacrament of the Present Moment*. Doesn't that say it all? Yesterday's sun doesn't warm us, he says, neither does tomorrow's. Only the sun of today gives us light and heat. In the same way, we can only receive God today. He says it's not easy, we have to train ourselves to be confined to the present. In one of his letters he wrote: 'Try not to let apprehension about the future or regret about the past flood over into your present living and make you miserable.'

But how do you do that? By doing it. By simply practising again and again being in the present moment. By saying 'Now' to yourself as you drive the car, then watching the landscape open into amazing beauty because instead of thinking about other things you are being totally aware of it. By letting your eyes see what they see, without words or thoughts. The more I dip into Tolle's book *The Power of Now* the more I see that so much of what he is recommending is what we experience when we are caught up in music or art. It's also related to meditation. People ask 'How do you begin to meditate?' and some meditators will say 'Concentrate on your breathing' and others will say 'Repeat a word over and over'. But these are all just methods of stilling your mind by getting it into the present moment. Telling yourself 'Now!' is just as good. It's also multi-purpose. Most people shut their eyes in meditation, but the practice of the present moment is larger than that, and can take place in normal everyday life, while driving, or walking, even while talking with people.

This practice of being totally in the present moment is doubly valuable in that it is prayer ('heaven in ordinarie ... the soul's blood', as the poet George Herbert called it) for the Christian – and probably for the Jew and the Muslim also – but it belongs equally to those who are uncomfortable with the words 'God' or 'prayer'.

Someone with experience of the 12-step programme of Alcoholics Anonymous tells me that the practice of 'Now' is effective in escaping from addiction. Using the word 'Power' is no exaggeration on Tolle's part. To be truly in the present moment is an incredible way out of stress, anxiety, depression. Turning off the thinking brain, and being aware of what all your senses are experiencing – sight, sound, touch, taste, smell – can bring relief within seconds. Which is more than you can say for psychotherapy or even drug therapy. And it's free, and it can do you no harm. You could try it now...

14

Growing and Eating Food is
Communing with the Divine

*The author visits Páirc a' Tobair, a 24-acre 'earth
learning' community run by a small number of Sisters of
Mercy in Rosscarbery [24 May 2008]*

Nuns aren't what they used to be. We know that most
of them now wear ordinary clothes like the rest of us.
But there are also great changes in what they are doing.

On the edge of Rosscarbery is Páirc a' Tobair, a 24-acre
'earth learning' community. For the past nine years a small
number of Sisters of Mercy have been living there, growing
their own organic vegetables and fruits, and planting trees and
wild flowers. There are several such projects around the
country. The largest is probably An Tairseach in Co.Wicklow,
run by Dominicans (www.ecocentrewicklow.com), but there
are other smaller ones at Mallow and Portumna established
by Mercy and Presentation Sisters.

Here in West Cork the land at Páirc a' Tobair was already owned by the local convent and was rented to local
farmers. Originally it was four or five fields, later made into
one big field. Now the Sisters are planting trees around the
edges of the field, and a strip of them across the middle also.
In all, they have planted about 7,000 native hedgerow and
woodland trees. Some of the trees such as hazel and ash will

be for coppicing in future. A young man called Dominic, keen on permaculture, established much of the initial plantings.

At present there are three Sisters there full time: Kathy Cunningham, Maria Hayes and Margaret Twomey. I went to see them on a wonderful spring day, and was treated with beautiful hospitality. They live in a simple wooden house on a hillside overlooking the water. The gardens are a delight, with fruit bushes and flowers and vegetables often growing together. There are hens, and an impressive polytunnel. There is a memorial grove, where people can plant a tree for a loved one who has died. None of the Sisters has horticultural training, though two of them grew up on farms in the days when farming was still very mixed. 'The learning is in the doing,' Sr Margaret says, as we walk the acres.

But these are not simply pleasure gardens. The overall vision of Páirc a' Tobair is to learn to live in a compassionate relationship with all of life and the whole earth community. This involves recognition of the interconnectedness of all created things, and the dependence of all creatures on the well-being of the planet.

The Sisters talk about the big issues. Increasing concern with global warming is making people realise that one way forward is the planting of our own food. Places like Cuba, China and Europe are leading the way. Even in cities people are finding small patches for growing. But can there ever be enough food for all when the population is swelling so rapidly? Population growth and poverty are linked, and they are both connected with the oil crisis. One of the Sisters says:

'Food is more than just what keeps us alive – it is commun-
ing with the divine.'

The leadership of the Order was very open to this project. And this openness is part of the great changes that are
happening. In the past, Orders were 'Mother Bountiful'.
They had money, they had houses, they had power. From
the time of the Famine onwards, they ran the schools, and
the hospitals.

But the revelations of abuse in religious institutions
changed all that.

Sr Kathy says: 'It was a very painful process. What was in
us, we asked, that led us to do those things? But in the end it
meant that we came off our pedestal of power. We realised
that we are the same as everyone else. Which was wonderful.'

Will 'the religious life' survive? The Sisters aren't sure.
'Religious orders used to be huge institutions – infantile, and
oppressive,' they say. In the past if there was a suitable person they would be made a postulant, brought into the novi-
tiate, and be taught all they needed to know. Eventually they
would take vows for life. Now convents are closing. Now
such a person would be encouraged simply to be around,
and take part in things. 'We would be learning from them at
least as much as they are learning from us.' The religious
Orders now have very participative leadership, much more
so than in the institutional church. 'We can challenge our
leadership.'

The real question, they say, is not the future of the religious life but the future of human life. 'If there is any hope
for religious life it lies in engagement with the concerns of

our time,' Sr Maria says. Most Orders have made some statement along ecological lines. The Páirc a' Tobair statement is of commitment to the land, and to life that has taken millions of years to evolve. 'We are not about producing things, marketing things.'

'A lot of it has to do with our idea of God,' Sr Kathy says. 'The kind of God we worship determines how we relate' – to people and to nature. She guesses that if we see God as a controlling figure then we will try to control the world around us. But if we see a God who needs us then we will work together with people and the natural world.

Visitors are welcomed at Páirc a' Tobair. Sometimes they come from Myross Wood when there is a retreat there, and other Mercy Sisters like to visit. Church groups? I ask. Not many, they say. Schools? 'We're more than happy to show them around.'

But the most popular part of the work at the Páirc is the Sisters' celebrations at the summer and winter solstices and the spring and autumn equinoxes. They began them seven years ago. 'Song and dance, fire and food' is the shape of the celebration. 'There is ritual, and sharing, and an awareness of the changing of the seasons.' Food is brought and shared. Poetry and music are often brought and shared too. All sorts of people arrive, including men and women who think their children need more experience of spirituality, and even those who would call themselves atheists. 'The emphasis is on our dependency on the earth, and giving thanks. Some of the atheists seem to have the greatest sense of wonder.'

'People say they're glad there's a place like this here.'

15

What Sort of God is it that They Don't Believe In?

The author is keenly aware of the uncertainty caused by each of us having a different image of what we call God
[7 June 2008]

In the past, people who didn't believe in God kept fairly quiet about it. But not now. Now people like Richard Dawkins are putting out great numbers of books about their disbelief. As a result, God and no-God are much discussed, at least in the media even if not in the supermarket and the street.

A Christian leader is reported to have said recently that we all have doubts. So couldn't we all, he said, believers and non-believers, begin by talking about our doubts? Couldn't the believers' doubt become the basis for dialogue with the non-believers?

Admitting that all is not certainty for Christians is a good start. But the trouble with that as a recipe for dialogue is that most of the atheists that I know – and some of them are very forceful atheists – don't *doubt* that God exists, they reckon they *know* there is no such being. No room for dialogue there. To enter into dialogue means that you want to find a middle ground with the other side. Most of the atheists that I know have no desire at all to reach agreement with a Christian like me. On the contrary, they keenly want to convert me to their own viewpoint!

So can we dialogue at all? 'God' versus 'no-God' is so black and white that we surely have to find a different route to making our own ideas more credible to non-believers. To put it all in a different light, a more apparently logical light.

One possibility is to ask ourselves what we mean by that word 'God', and see if there is any common ground about the meaning of life without using that word. The word is only a word that stands for something we experience as a reality. When I was young I saw one of Ingmar Bergman's films in which the characters, speaking Swedish, went on and on about a being called 'Gird'. I remember thinking I was glad I wasn't Swedish because I didn't think I could really pray if I had to use the word 'Gird'. On the other hand, the word is a lot better in a lot of other languages. 'Dieu' (French) is a beautiful sound. 'Allah' (Arabic) is gentle. 'Dia' (Irish) is appealing and 'Duw' (Welsh) is passionate. I wonder, is our relationship to the divine influenced by the word we use?

Whatever about that, it is only a word, not the reality itself. Yet when we say that we believe in God, we are instantly setting up a pre-packaged image in the minds of the people we're talking to. They think they know exactly what we mean. But do they?

In my years of parish ministry I've often encountered people who have said, 'I don't believe in God.' So I've asked them, 'What sort of God don't you believe in?' Out comes a horrible caricature, a god of anger and thou-shalt-nots, a god of power that is expected to produce miracles on demand, but instead kills innocent people. And I say, 'I don't believe in that God either.'

We probably each have a different image of what we call by that one word, while imagining that we're all talking about the same thing. It's no good the Bible-based believer saying, 'But God has been revealed to us in the scriptures,' because, whether we intend it or not, we each have a different take on what is written there. To put it at its most simple, some see a God of love revealed and some see a God of righteous anger.

Discussion is further confused when the figure of Jesus is brought in. Now I know that in traditional Christian theology Jesus is God. There are all sorts of different ways of understanding that, but many people say 'Jesus' when they mean God, and 'God' when they mean Jesus. Pity the poor atheists, trying to cope with that!

I wonder is it unfair to say that we clergy are a lot to blame for people throwing out God, on the grounds that we have said altogether far too much about God, made God far too concrete. Not just human-shaped, Jesus-shaped. But 'God says this-and-this,' we say. 'God wants that-and-that,' we assert. The more we act as if we know all about God, the more likelihood there is of that self-selected image being rejected. Some have caused a lot of harm and hatred and grief by using scriptural passages to boost their own particular idea of God, as when they say the Bible shows that God forbids same-sex relationships – see Leviticus 18:22. (If that is so, God also forbids going near the altar if you have a skin blemish – Lev. 21:18. And eating Clonakilty pudding – Lev. 17:12.)

St Augustine said something huge when he said, 'If you understand God, it is not God.' If we're going to quote the Bible at all we can go for what the early writers reckon God told Moses when Moses asked, 'Who are you?' Translations vary, but it comes out as something like, 'I am that I am,' or 'I am what is.' No name, just 'is', 'am'. That's wonderful. Like watching a bird instead of trying to name it. When we name something we are attempting to own it, to control it. That 'I am' throws our minds inside out, beyond owning and controlling, beyond understanding, into pure experiencing.

Where's the common ground then, for Christians and atheists, and humanists too, if Christians for the sake of dialogue lay aside the G-word? Could it be in what the nineteenth century American writer Emerson called the over-soul? The link between human beings, the sense that we are all somehow inter-related, and that we need each other? The twentieth century enlarged on it, slowly recognising that we are all related to everything that is. The human world and the natural world, all inter-dependent. You can picture it as a great cloud wrapping the universe together. Or see it, if you want, as the spirit of life. Or you could call it 'the ground of our being'. Or, if it seems good to do so, you can call it 'God'.

16

Singing 'Oh How Beautiful' and Sitting in the Shade

The author sees the image of God in the garden as very
strong and persistent though it may be seen as a
primitive idea [21 June 2008]

'And they heard the voice of the Lord, walking in the garden in the cool of the day.' This lovely sentence, from the first book of the Bible, is about Adam and Eve. Originally written in Hebrew, there are lots of different translations of it. The Catholic version, in the Jerusalem Bible, has 'The man and his wife heard the sound of Yahweh God walking in the garden in the cool of the day.' The Jewish version, in the New JPS Translation, says: 'They heard the sound of the Lord God moving about in the garden at the breezy time of day.'

However you translate it, the image is beautiful in its simplicity. These chapters, two to four, of the Book of Genesis, containing the story of the 'first' man and woman and their offspring, are among the oldest passages of the Bible. They were probably written nine centuries BCE, or before Jesus was born. So that's nearly thirty centuries ago. (The first chapter, with the story of God creating the heavens and the earth, is much newer, probably written down a mere 500 years BCE.) Their idea of God in those times was clearly very human-shaped. Human enough to want to wait until the cool of the evening, the time of day when there would be a nice breeze after the day's heat.

It may be a primitive idea, but this image of the God in the garden is a very strong and persistent one. The beautiful hymn 'Walking in the garden' gives three different garden images, from Adam to Mary Magdalen. There are lines by Dorothy Gurney (1858-1932) that, when I was young, used to be quoted by misty-eyed old ladies:

'The kiss of the sun for pardon,
The song of the birds for mirth.
One is nearer God's Heart in a garden
Than anywhere else on earth.'

When I was a teenager we used to laugh at that verse. Now I'm a misty-eyed old lady myself I understand it.

Gardens have been used through the centuries as symbols of happiness and innocent joy. Frances Bacon, in the seventeenth century, said that God planted the first garden and that a garden is 'the purest of human pleasures'. In our own time, Joni Mitchell sang, 'We are stardust / We are golden / And we got to get ourselves / Back to the garden.' Bing Crosby even seems to have picked up the nostalgia of that story about God walking in the garden when he sang: 'In the cool, cool, cool of the evening / Tell 'em I'll be there / In the cool, cool, cool of the evening / Save your pappy a chair...'

But gardens are only a small, special part of the natural world. Satish Kumar, editor of the magazine *Resurgence*, has said that nature is his 'guide and cathedral'. He loves walking.

When you walk, he says, you are in touch with the earth, wasps and insects and all. In a car you are disconnected, but when you walk you 'connect yourself'. Anyone who has ever walked a route that they normally drive will recognise the truth of that. In a car, what we pass is like the backdrop in an old fashioned film, or the painted scenery in a theatre. But when we're on foot, suddenly everything – the ditches beside the road, the fields, the houses – is very close-up, and very real. It's as if we're part of it. As of course we are. And, as Kumar pointed out in a recent interview with John Vidal, that is a spiritual experience. 'The ordinary is the extraordinary,' he says.

Some years ago, on holiday in another country, I went on Sunday to the local church. It was probably a very good church and maybe it was a good service. All I know is that it seemed like a meaningless noise. I wished I hadn't come and I couldn't wait to get out. Escaping, at the end of the service, to the outside world was wonderful. And even though the sky was overcast, walking along the nearby seashore restored me. I hadn't found God at all in that building, but as I walked God was everywhere.

And haven't we all moved on from the time when divinity was locked up in church buildings, found only on Sundays and holy days? Now we recognise it in nature, and also in art and poetry and music and film. Not just in the old classical works, and not just in 'religious' music and art. The boundaries between 'religious' and 'secular' are dissolving. Only a few decades ago it seemed quite radical to discover spiritual themes in secular works of art. Or to find theology in films, even general release films. Now everyone seems to be doing it.

Poetry has always been a vehicle for religious ideas, and has constantly blurred the distinction between secular and sacred. There are churches where a piece of modern poetry will be read as a 'third reading', acknowledging that divine inspiration is not limited to the Bible.

And of course we find the divine in each other. In human beings everywhere. 'We come to God through each other,' one of my friends likes to say, and most of us would probably agree. But it's not one-sided. The other side is the scary realisation that other people come to God through us.

It's the same with art and music and all those other things. Haven't we some sort of responsibility for giving as well as just sitting back happily and receiving? Rudyard Kipling, in his poem 'The Glory of the Garden', says '... such gardens are not made / By singing 'Oh, how beautiful' and sitting in the shade...'

If you are following the West Cork Garden Trail this summer, think of those who do the work. Kipling goes on:

> 'Then seek your job with thankfulness and work till
>   further orders,
> If it's only netting strawberries or killing slugs on
>   borders;
> And when your back stops aching and your hands
>   begin to harden,
> You will find yourself a partner in the Glory of the
>   Garden.'

17

Tell Me I'm Rubbish and I'll
Act Like Rubbish

*The author believes that if we feel loved and
respected then we can love and respect other people,
and ourselves too [5 July 2008]*

One of the things that most impressed me when I came
to Ireland to work was the local community college.
Not just the fact that the buildings were sited so wonderfully
at the water's edge, or even that – amazingly – sailing was on
the curriculum. What surprised and delighted me above all
was the way staff and students related to each other. In English schools at teenage level I'd seen two sorts of teenage
behaviour that appalled me. One was a sort of bowing and
scraping attitude, designed to placate the enemy and not
draw attention. YesSirNoSir. The other was jeering rude-
ness, born of boredom and designed to provoke conflict
with the teachers.

It was hard to believe the difference at the college here.
As the local rector I went in once a week to do some religious education with the handful of young people who
weren't Catholic. Going to the classroom, I'd see a teenager
and a staff member walking towards each other down the
corridor. From past experience I'd have expected them to
sneak past each other with eyes averted, to avoid any sort

of unnecessary encounter. Instead, they were quite likely to stop and talk about some practical matter, in a normal conversational tone. No cringing deference, and no aggression either. But like one human being talking to another. I thought it was wonderful, and I still do.

Another thing that delighted my family and me when we moved here was the way young people talk to older people. On a bus, schoolchildren often talk to the driver when they're getting on or off. If an older person says something to them in the street they answer not just with a curt Yes or No (or worse), and not with nervous politeness either, but with a relaxed normality.

Ireland is a gentler country, where people are less ready to hurt each others' feelings. More ready, it seems, to respect each other. This applies not only to relationships between students and staff, and young and old, but also between men and women. In Britain and America you often hear wolf whistles in the street, but in our twelve years here I've only ever heard a public wolf-whistle once, and I'd guess with some certainty that the whistler was not Irish. In other countries, even when men have adopted politically correct attitudes to women, there is still somehow an awareness that they are being politically correct. That has the effect of making a woman constantly aware that she is a woman and that the man she is talking to is a man. It's as if there's an under-the-surface smirking going on. It doesn't feel like that here.

When I was being interviewed for my job, we were halfway through a two hour interview before I suddenly realised I was the only woman in the room. We were talking like human beings, not 'We're all men and you're a woman!' And in case you're thinking all of this is just because I'm grey-haired now, I'll add that it's not just me who sees it this way. I've asked younger woman who have lived abroad, and they agree that the relationship between women and men is more relaxed here.

So what is it that makes it all so much more pleasant here? I think it's that important word 'respect'. Whether it is some aspect of Irish history that is at the root of it, or whether it is the effect of a Catholic culture, I don't know. But religion should have had something to do with it. Jesus said that all the religious laws could be summed up in the two old Jewish laws: love God, love your neighbour. That word 'love' has come to us through many translations, Aramaic, Greek, Latin, sixteenth century English, and more. It's an all-purpose sort of word, and can mean different things in different settings. Love your neighbour? – but what if a neighbour is a real problem? You can love without always liking. God loves us? – that could sound hopelessly sentimental. The word in that setting is better translated as being 'loving kindness'. Whatever, it is what respect is built out of. It suggests knowing someone, and still caring about them no matter what you know about them. Psalm 138/139 is a great image of this. It begins, 'Lord, you have searched me out and known me, You ...are acquainted with all my ways...' and it goes on to a beautiful description of God's care: 'If I take the wings of the morning, and settle at the furthest limits of the sea, even there your hand shall lead me, and your right hand shall hold me fast.'

If we feel loved and respected then we can love and respect other people, and ourselves too. We talk a lot about people having 'low self-esteem'. That's not just a problem for the pages of the women's magazines. So much of the crime and violence in society is down to too many people having low self-esteem. Put simply, tell me I'm rubbish and I'll act like rubbish. That way I'll get power and then I'll feel all right.

I talked to the principal of that community college about the good atmosphere I had found there. He agreed that not all Irish schools would be the same. It can be different in inner city areas of social deprivation and, interestingly, in some private schools where the students feel superior to the staff because of the high fees their parents are paying.

I asked him how the good atmosphere was built in his college. It was there right from the first few years after the school was built, he said, and is passed on from year to year. Students coming in from other places sometimes find it strange, and have difficulty sorting out where the boundaries are. They may for a while be cheeky, until they get the sense of it. It is all based on respect that is mutual. The new Student Code of Conduct, drawn up by staff and students together, begins, 'Show respect and courtesy to everyone…'

What we all really need, to feel good about ourselves, is the simple respect that is a form of love. We learn to give it *to* others by receiving it *from* others. And if we all felt good about ourselves we wouldn't need to have power over each other. What a peaceful world it would be.

18

The Church's Attitude to Homo-sexuality: The New Apartheid

The author looks at the problems facing the
Anglican Church as the diocesan bishops gather for
their Lambeth Conference [26 July 2008]

The great thing about the world-wide Anglican Church (the Church of Ireland is part of it) has always been that it is a broad church. Broad enough to include 'low church' evangelicals and 'high church' Anglo-Catholics. People who like worship to be plain and simple, in unadorned buildings and with no fancy clothes for the clergy, and people who really only feel at home when there are candles and incense on the altar, and silk and lace on the clergy. Broad enough to include quite large differences in the way God, and the Bible, are understood. Conservative traditionalists, and progressive liberals. Broad enough to include black and white and gay and lesbian and heterosexual and everyone in between. Broad enough to call itself not so much 'Protestant' as 'Catholic *and* Reformed'.

Anglicans of every variety were proud of that breadth of tolerance. But now all that is under threat. The Church appears to be in danger of splitting because of different views on sexuality.

All the diocesan bishops of the Anglican Communion of Churches from around the world should be at the Lambeth

Conference, which is taking place in England now until August 3 under the leadership of the Archbishop of Canterbury, Dr Rowan Williams. The 2008 Lambeth Conference (they happen every ten years) has two aims, Dr Williams has said. To help the bishops to help the Church grow, and to strengthen their sense of a shared Anglican identity. It is sad and ironic then, that a number bishops have not even turned up for the conference.

Instead, some of them had their own conference in Jerusalem last month. The Global Anglican Future Conference (Gafcon) drew some 300 bishops and archbishops from places like Australia and Africa and England. Together they set up the Fellowship of Confessing Anglicans (Foca). This is to be a network for the millions of Anglican clergy and lay people who are unhappy with the increasingly open and liberal attitudes that they see in the rest of the Church. Attitudes to matters like homosexuality, and women priests and bishops. Those who join Foca will have no women clergy, no gay clergy and no same-sex unions. They plan to 'reassert the authority of the Bible'.

Dr Williams has called the absence of those bishops 'a great grief ... because we need their voice and they need ours in learning Christ together'.

One or two of our Church of Ireland bishops may have had misgivings about accepting their invitation to the Conference, but it is good to know that in the end all of them decided to go. What mainly decided the Gafcon bishops to boycott the Lambeth Conference was one man. A gentle, prayerful man, a much-loved pastor from the USA, Gene Robinson is Bishop of New Hampshire and he is gay. Openly gay, living with his partner, and even so, chosen by his people to be their bishop. But not all of the 77 million Anglicans in the world were happy with their choice. For many traditionalists it was final confirmation that they had to distance themselves from such actions.

Now the attitude to homosexuality in some sections of the Church has been compared to apartheid. Former archbishop Desmond Tutu has said that he is ashamed of his homophobic Anglican Communion.

The big question is, will that distancing become total breakaway? Just as the priority for any bishop is the unity of the church that is under his or her leadership, so Archbishop Rowan Williams sees his main task as holding together the world-wide church. He has made so many concessions to the conservatives and the traditionalists that there is now a rising tide of voices asking him to trust his own liberal inclinations and give no more ground.

It would of course be sad if a number of clergy and lay people left the Anglican Church and set up on their own. But hasn't that been happening all through history? In medieval times the Christian Church split into eastern and western factions: Eastern Orthodox, based in Constantinople, and Roman Catholic, based in Rome. Then the Anglicans and Lutherans and Calvinists all separated from the Roman Church in the sixteenth century. A few hundred years later the Methodists split from the Anglicans, just as Presbyterianism grew out of Calvinism. If these new Anglican breakaways set up their own Church it too will probably divide again. Those who object to theological liberalism come from the two extremes of the Church, the conservative evangelicals and the Anglo-Catholics. Some of the Anglo-Catholics are considering 'going over to Rome' and that would be unthinkable to the evangelicals.

One of the deep-down issues in all this is authority. The fact that the centre of the Anglican world is in England is a problem in itself. It has overtones of colonialism, even though the Archbishop of Canterbury has no binding power over Anglican churches beyond his own diocese. In the hope of preventing a split, a new Covenant has been proposed which would give Canterbury almost papal authority. Our own Bishop of Cork, Paul Colton, has warned that that would compromise the autonomy of the Church of Ireland and others. Meanwhile, the Gafcon group are saying they will no longer recognise the authority of the Archbishop of Canterbury. Dr Williams has responded, in an unusually challenging tone, by saying that Gafcon lacks legitimacy, integrity – and authority. At the same time Tom Wright, Bishop of Durham, has called the authority that Gafcon is claiming 'deeply offensive.' What is significant here is that he is a leading conservative.

What has all this bitter arguing to do with that first century man called Jesus, whose radical call to a new way of living lies behind this vast structure we call Christianity? Rowan Williams has called the bishops to find a common mind. His own prayer and hope for the Conference, he said, 'is not that after two weeks we will find a solution to all our problems but we shall … in some sense find the trust in God and one another that will give us the energy to change in the way God wants us to change … individually and as a Communion.'

19

The Sun and the Heavens, Angels and Archangels

The author says that while our reliance on the Celtic tiger has made a bit of a mess of life on this island, a renewal of Celtic Christianity could just possibly replace the mess with a bit of heaven on earth [2 August 2008]

'I will kindle my fire this morning
In the presence of the holy angels of heaven ...
God kindle in my heart within
A flame of love to my neighbour,
To my foe, to my friend, to my kindred all ...'

It was prayers like these, homely and beautiful, that made the modern world fall in love with what they called 'Celtic Christianity'. Somewhere around the late 1970s the bookshops of England and America began to fill up with books about the religion of Ireland and Scotland and Wales as it was for hundreds of years after Christianity began in these islands in the third century. A wonderful, simple religion it seemed, centred on an awareness of the presence of God in all of life, and on living in harmony with nature. There were books about the simple Celtic lifestyle, anthologies of Celtic prayers, and poetry-and-picture books showing high crosses, and rugged Skellig-style steps, and beehive monastic cells.

This interest in all things Celtic blossomed and flourished into the early years of the new century. Adventurous churches held Celtic services. Retreat houses and monasteries offered Celtic retreats. The Church of Ireland very nearly included a Celtic form of service in its new Book of Common Prayer. The fascination became commercialised, if it wasn't already: cathedral shops shone with Celtic jewellery and Celtic colouring books.

We learned a whole new way of looking at the history of Christianity in Britain and Ireland. The Church had been firmly established by the year 400. Later, Columba and the other saints from Ireland had evangelised Scotland and northern England, and St Augustine from Rome had been working away in southern England. Northern Christianity was monastic, Celtic, while the Church in the south was bureaucratic, Roman. It might have gone on like that if they hadn't met up at Whitby, in Yorkshire, in the year 664, and had a disagreement about how to calculate the date of Easter. St Hilda, Abbess of Whitby, and others, decided to go with the way it was done in Rome. The monks of Lindisfarne disagreed with that, and went off to the Scottish island of Iona, and later to Ireland. That was the end, we were told, of Celtic Christianity in Britain. Now it was all contained in Ireland.

But the fascination with Celtic history was blown up so big it had to burst. The whole thing was a load of nonsense, we learned last year. We Celts – Irish, Scots, Welsh, Bretons, etc – had not fought our way nobly across Europe, making richly-patterned pots and coins as we went. We were here all the time. Sitting around on the edge of the Atlantic ocean, quietly fishing and hunting. Simply surviving.

Only the wealthy among us got into 'Celtic art', buying and copying it from central Europe.

Even the Whitby saga turned out to be a serious over-simplification. The demise of the monastic model of Christianity was much more gradual, and much less romantic. We'd been had. You could almost see the Celtic jewellery being put under the counter and the books of Celtic prayers being remaindered. It was enough to have deflated the whole Celtic Christianity cult.

But maybe it hasn't – and maybe that is very good. The style of religion that we were attributing to the non-existent Celts is beautiful. If we were moving in that direction, why stop? It has its own validity in history, and there is so much in it that we need at this time.

What most attracts people is its simple and natural acceptance of the divine as something interwoven with everyday life. A loving and nurturing sort of God, a reality that upholds everything we do and everything we are. So that it is natural to connect with that God when you are wanting your work to come out right, or wanting someone you love to travel safely. That connecting is prayer in the very best sense. Not a quick gabble of words, or a mindless gesture, but a real getting in touch with the source of all life.

Another attraction is that those early Christians had such a positive and affirmative view of us human beings. They didn't believe in Original Sin, for a start. That was the idea that, because Adam and Eve sinned, so we are all corrupt from birth and in need of salvation. It came basically from St Augustine, who put it down mostly to lust. The early Christians in Ireland tended instead to follow the teachings of Pelagius, who said there was no way that a human soul created out of divine goodness could be born stained. The writings of Pelagius were optimistic about the human capacity to move towards total goodness. And, like the writings of St Patrick in the same era, they were full of wonderful images of God, images of the sun and the heavens, of angels and archangels.

These images are not there to be dissected and analysed. They are metaphor, poetry, mystery, wonder, delight. Even the image of the Trinity, of God as three-in-one, which can cause such problems for anyone trying to take it too literally, becomes acceptable as poetry. As poetry, it is a way of saying that God is not an isolated aloneness, but relationship, divine-human community, love in action.

This god-centred way of life was not run by a distant authority, as it was in Britain then, but was based on local community. Communities centred on local monasteries, where people went to worship. The monks, who produced their own food and herbs and medicines, usually offered care not just for the soul but for the body also. And not just for the local people but for the travellers and the strangers as well.

There's another reason why all of this is important to us now. As the earliest form of the Christian faith on this island, it is bigger than all our subsequent divisions. It is beyond sectarianism. It belongs to all of us — and to the travellers and the strangers also. At a time like this, when we are beginning to realise that our reliance on the Celtic tiger has made a bit of a mess of life on this island, a renewal of Celtic Christianity could just possibly replace the mess with a bit of heaven on earth.

20

Dropping Religion and Going for Spirituality

The author wonders how the churches should relate to people who say they want to be spiritual but have no time for religion [23 August 2008]

The buzz question in certain circles now is, 'What is the difference between religion and spirituality?'

The answer is usually something about religion being down, and spirituality being up. 'Religion' now means institutional religion: buildings, finance, clergy, doctrine and rules. It is seen as closed up and lifeless. And spirituality? Often it is defined as a search for the meaning of life, especially where there is a sense that we are more than just our physical bodies. Our local poet-priest Michael McCarthy has described it as 'where the divine and the human connect'. Unlike religion, spirituality is seen as open and full of life, larger than the church, and the hope for the future. And the common feeling is that people are turning away from 'religion' and going for 'spirituality'.

A modern Hindu monk, Swami Agnivesh, has controversially said that religions – all religions – are based on territory, conformity, self-interest and exclusion. They put down the prophetic and critical elements in order to preserve their clerical status. Spirituality, he says, is different. It spreads outwards from the individual to embrace the whole world. It brings change. It connects the salvation of the individual with the transformation of society.

Many Christians are saying similar things. They are saying that institutional religion, organised religion, has become turned in on itself, bogged down in its internal problems, obsessed with its own survival. It has lost the ability to connect us with God, the divine, the numinous, or however you choose to put it. Yet this connection is what increasing numbers of people are looking for now.

All religions began from this connection of the human with the divine, the deep sense of a Reality greater than time or space. They began in awe and wonder, with hearts and minds lifted up into the heavens. But over the centuries very human concerns pulled it all down to earthly practicalities.

Gatherings that began in the open air or in people's homes became so large that special buildings were erected. Buildings needed money. At first money came easily, from the generosity of the worshippers' enthusiasm. Then, as the faith communities grew, it wasn't enough for the local sailmaker or fisherman or housewife to take the lead at gatherings. It became a full-time job and that needed more money from the community. Then a treasurer would be needed to look after the money. And so the practical work expanded. Parish administrator, bishop's secretary, diocesan architect. Lawyers, accountants, communications officers.

Now, in the twenty-first century, so many of our Christian churches are worried about the huge loads they are carrying. Where will the money come from to support the church of the future? What will happen to all the buildings as fewer people fill them? Where will the clergy come from, to lead the people? If the answers are obvious, the church authorities don't want to hear them.

That's the down side of the future. The up side is more misty. Where are they going, the increasing numbers of spiritual seekers? Many of them have had no contact at all with religious practice. Others, who have been faithful members of the churches, have given up and walked away from them in disillusionment, frustration and despair. Some of those will have found something that feeds them, but many are spiritually starving still.

You could say that there are three options for the future of Christianity. One is that all the seekers will, in the end, find a home in Buddhism or yogic meditation or the rituals of Wicca or nature worship. Meanwhile, the churches will keep their heads down in the sand and continue with their present membership as it gets older and dwindles and dies, and then Christianity will cease to exist.

The second possibility is that the seekers will gradually realise the strength of their numbers, while at the same time recognising the value of the Jesus-story, and grow their own version of Christianity, open to all. They will become a new church, or they will draw in all the living Christians from the old churches and become the ongoing Christian tradition.

The third is that the churches, driven by events, will change and survive. That they will let the Spirit back in, and will open up, and change, and blossom into new life. Change from money-based businesses, with property and employees, to faith-centred communities living in the presence of God and working for the well-being of the world. That third option would be very difficult, involving a great letting-go, of power and status and security. But isn't letting-go just exactly what all the religions call us to do?

It would be tragic if Christianity were to die for want of the courage to change. Ultimately, the world needs religion *and* spirituality. Religion at its worst is terrible, as the Inquisition and the Holocaust remind us. But spirituality can open the door to evil, too, if it is an escape from reality. If we all go off with the fairies we will end in a bog of sentimentality that has no way of coping with suffering and death and disaster. I used to worry, when I was in parish ministry, about the people who would come happily to church on Easter Day but would never attend a Good Friday service. Facing up to crucifixion and death is a ritual of great spiritual health-giving, and the only way to get through to Resurrection.

The swing away from institutional religion is something that was waiting to happen, for many reasons, historical and administrative. But if, at its best, it is the means by which we share our spirituality and build a better world out of it, it surely deserves to be saved. The question is, can we call on spirituality to redeem religion?

We have such treasures to draw on from the past. The whole Jesus-tradition is almost enough in itself. But we also have centuries of glorious and challenging art and music and scripture and poetry. We have traditions of worship that open the way into the presence of God. We have the knowledge of generations of saintly people, and millions of inspirational stories. And we have treasures of the present moment to draw on, too. Nature, relationships, concern for others. They feed us as individuals and as communities, and send us out trailing the divine into the daily life of the world.

How then should the churches relate to people who say that want to be spiritual but have no time for religion? This is a deep and serious challenge, and one that needs to be faced not tomorrow or next year but now.

21

Funeral Planning: Easing the Loss for the Family

The author believes that planning your own funeral could greatly ease the loss of you for your family and friends
[6 September 2008]

Irish funerals are so good. That was one of my best discoveries when I first moved from being a city-centre Vicar in the Church of England to being a rural Rector in the Church of Ireland. This country knows how to deal with death. An Irish colleague who has worked in England refers to the 'body-out-of-sight' style of English funerals, but says that in Ireland, 'There is no way you can pretend a death hasn't happened.'

What's good about Irish funerals is the way they surround and support the bereaved. The way they begin to happen, in four or five different stages, straight after the death. And the way they involve the whole community and take place within its familiar buildings. (The exception would be those that are held in the Dublin crematorium.)

In contrast, the great majority of English funerals now take place in a crematorium, a building that must seem unfamiliar and impersonal to most of the people attending. Not three days after the death, but a week or more. You could say this has the advantage that family members from far away have a good change of travelling to be there in time for it. But the downside is that that week is seven long days of emptiness and unreality for the immediate family. It numbs them. 'It'll be alright when the funeral's over,' they say. Nothing happens between the death and the funeral service, unless the family ask to see the body, privately, at the funeral home. There are no gatherings for prayer at the death-bed, no open coffin, no community presence at the removal, no crowds walking the coffin to the church. When the funeral finally does come, there will normally be only a small number of people present. Sometimes care-home staff attend the funerals of their residents because otherwise there will be no-one in the crematorium except the clergyperson, the organist and the funeral director.

In Ireland death is seen as part of life, not something hidden away and frightening. Small children are accustomed to it by being taken to removals. It's all very healthy and therapeutic for everyone.

I can think of only one way in which our funerals could be even better. That would be if more of us planned our own. It's fine for the family and friends to meet with the clergy and choose the hymns together, and maybe the readings. But how much better it is when the person leading the service can say, 'Now we're going to sing his favourite hymn,' or 'This next hymn was one she had at her wedding, so she wanted us to sing it now.' When that happens the congregation can feel really connected to the one they are mourning.

I've led several funerals where not only the hymns but the readings as well were chosen by the people themselves, and the difference that has made to family and friends and neighbours is hard to exaggerate. Most often the planning has been done when they were already seriously ill, and the time when we sat together and talked about the possibilities has been very moving. But in other instances the choices have been made by men and women in good health. Their wishes have been written down, and their families or friends told where that paper is kept.

It can be quite rewarding to decide which hymns come closest to what you feel about God and the world and yourself. If some you choose are unusual you might suggest that the congregation be led in a practice before the service begins. Which Bible readings speak to you most inspiringly? You may be able to have other readings also. There is so much choice, from spiritual classics to modern poetry, or significant passages of prose. There are books and books of amazingly good prayers. If you don't have any yourself your priest or minister can probably lend you some. And then there's music. You might ask for something on CD to be played: part of Mozart's Requiem, perhaps, or Bach, or Karl Jenkins. The monks of Glenstal are unlikely to be at your funeral but the sound of their beautiful Gregorian chant could be.

There have been difficulties sometimes when songs like the popular 'I Did it My Way' are requested by the family. The Catholic Bishop of Clogher recently called for a ban on popular songs at funerals, songs such as 'Goodbye My Lover' and U2's 'With or Without You'. The bishop said that personal poems and songs could be heard at the deceased's home. Some people could get upset about that. But it points to a larger question. Whose benefit is the funeral for?

All through Christian history the liturgy for the dead has found its meaning in resurrection. Because Jesus was raised from the dead, it says, we too shall be raised. The prayers, the readings, the hymns, are intended to focus on the belief that nothing, 'neither death, nor life, ... nor things present nor things to come ... will be able to separate us from the love of God in Christ Jesus our Lord.' All this, then, is what a funeral should be, theologically speaking. Not a prolonged eulogy about how lovely the departed was ('He/she would do anything for anyone') but a committing of them into God's keeping.

Yet there is also very definitely a pastoral, therapeutic aspect to a funeral. People are vulnerable at funerals, open to feelings not only of grief but often also of guilt ('I should have visited him more often,' 'I never really told her I loved her'). This is where prayers and hymns and readings chosen by the one who is gone can be very valuable, because they do seem to speak personally to the bereaved.

Don't overlook the practical details. My mother asked us to be sure her Missal, that we children had given her decades ago, was buried with her. You might want to specify that you have the simplest possible coffin, perhaps a biodegradeable one. That will save your relatives feeling they will be dishonouring you if they don't choose the one with the most carving on it, the most glitzy handles, the most gorgeous satin lining.

Planning your own funeral could greatly ease the loss of you for your family and friends.

22

Change Can Be Healthy but It Can Be Scary Too

The author is a member of the Open Christianity Network which provides an outlet for discussion on the future of Christianity [4 October 2008]

A sense of security is surely one of the benefits of religion. Let it rain, let it snow, let food prices go up and mortgages become impossible, let our newspapers fizz with stories of crime and corruption, but let a Christian step into a familiar church and the chances are that their blood pressure will fall and after a little while all the problems will be smaller. Religion is good for us, in general. People who have it tend to live longer than those who don't.

So we treasure that sense of security. And we are horri-
fied by anything that seems to threaten it. Change, for example. Will we change the way things are done in the church?
'Never!' Will we change the words of the liturgy or of the
Bible? 'If they were good enough for St Paul they're good
enough for me.' Will we change the building itself? 'I'd fight
that to my dying day.' All credit, then, to those congregations
who have been brave enough to make alterations when they
were necessary. It may not have been easy, but it is a mark of
their faith and trust in God that they decided to do it.

Not everything is good just because it's old. Or because
'that's the way we've always done it'. The needs of a community change, for one thing. What feeds one generation
may leave the next starving. And a quick glance at the history of religion will show us that people have experienced
the guidance of God as endlessly unfolding. Slavery is the
obvious example. For centuries perfectly good Christians
used to be engaged in it, and believed that God was quite
happy with that. And then – thunderbolts! – in the eight-
eenth century, they realised God was not at all happy with
it. It had to be abolished.

All sorts of new things are happening in religion, generally moving forward, occasionally moving backwards. But Ireland is sometimes a long way from anywhere else, and we are
not much touched by religious change. Is that good? My personal answer to that is Yes, where it means we are still a religious people with an awareness of the divine in our everyday
lives. But I'd also answer No, where it means we are un-
touched by all the hope-giving developments that are happening in other places.

In most of the English-speaking countries of the world there are 'Emerging Churches', 'Alternative Worship', café churches, base ecclesial churches, 'Progressive Spirituality', 'Fresh Expressions'. They are churches or groups that are learning together to express their faith in vital new ways. But in Ireland, where are these churches or groups?

If you have given up on the religion of your childhood but miss it; if you object to saying you believe what you don't believe; if you have found your own way into contact with the divine; if you are infuriated by the way the church runs itself; or you think it is concerned with all the wrong things – these 'emerging' groups may be your sort of people.

There are loads of websites for these movements. Any one of them may lead you on, through its Links, to others. You could start with www.emergingchurch.info or www.alternativeworship.org or www.dream.uk.net (while you're on that one, look for the blog called 'Jesus didn't talk to prostitutes'!)

There are clearly a lot of different ways of being 'alternative' church or 'emerging' church. Some of them are totally tied in with existing church communities, and clergy-organised, finding new ways to present the Gospel to new people. At the other extreme there are groups of lay people getting together across denominational boundaries and exploring new ways, radically simple, of being Christian.

The Alternative Worship website has a good section explaining how to build an alternative worship group. It's put together by Paul Roberts, who has been involved in this form of worship since 1993. You can't do it alone, he says. You need a group of people. Even then, it may take months

or years of meeting together, eating and drinking and exploring together, before you all feel ready. When the time
feels right, you need a venue.

'Are you going to go it alone,' Roberts asks, 'or are you
going to be part of some pre-existing Church grouping? The
alternative worship world is divided on this question: for
some groups, the world of established Christianity is the very
thing that they're trying to escape from. They don't want to
be part of someone else's project, with hidden agendas of
growing someone's church…. On the other hand, there are
also examples where alternative worship is successfully existing alongside more usual forms of church life. For this to
work, it is vital that the leadership and membership of the
wider church realise that the alternative worship setting is
'real church' in its own right, and allow it to exist as a discrete
congregation and develop its own ways of doing things.'

The Anglican and Methodist website, www.freshexpres-
sions.org.uk, has a directory of 686 alternative churches and
groups of all denominations. But it lists only one in the
whole of Ireland. That is the non-denominational (and wild)
Ikon, in Belfast (www.ikon.org.uk.) There may be others
they don't know about. There is a base ecclesial group near
Clonakilty, for one.

What Ireland does have, north and south, is the Open
Christianity Network (www.ocnireland.com). I'll declare an
interest here, as I've been involved with it from its beginning.
It's a talking shop, basically, for men and women of all denominations or none. They are people who are concerned
about the future of Christianity in Ireland, and want to find
others prepared to think outside the box from time to time.

To discuss matters of faith, belief, church organisation, whatever. At their meetings they might listen to a speaker, or
choose a particular subject or a new book to discuss. They
talk as equals, laity and clergy. Their views may vary widely,
but are heard with respect. It's proof that you can think later-
ally and still be a Christian, and it's a real lifeline for some.

23

Halloween – There Must Be a Better Way

*The author looks at attempts made to provide alternative
forms of Halloween and makes some further suggestions
[18 October 2008]*

Monsters and ghosts and devils and skulls, as hideous as
they can make them, are in all the shops now. The
stuff of nightmares. Luminous and ghastly, they fill the
shelves that a few weeks ago were full of soft baby toys and
dear little girly jewellery, all pink and lilac.

Am I imagining it, or are there increasing numbers of
people who are nervous of Halloween – especially in the big
cities? Worried about endless knocking and doorbell ringing.
Worried about the so-called tricks that may be played on
them if they don't hand over acceptable gifts to their small

(or not so small) visitors on that night. Older people will say it was never like this when they were young.

Some people have other concerns about Halloween. It's too Americanised, they say. Or, it's pagan. Or, it's a celebration of evil. Or they ask, why does it happen at the same time of year as All Saints day, and All Souls day? Could it be somehow different, could it be something better?

Before there was any Christianity in Ireland, the great festival of Samhain marked the end of summer and the storing of food for the winter months. Being at a turning point of the year, it was also a time when the boundary between the living and the dead was felt to be very thin. A time when the dead might come through again, and cause sickness in the animals or diseases in the crops. Bonfires were lit to keep them away, and fancy costumes and masks were worn to confuse them.

In the eighth century the church 'christianised' the festival, just as Easter and Christmas had been placed over other pagan festivals. The Pope took All Saints Day (All Hallows), which had been on May 13, and moved it to the first of November, to cover Samhain. In those times the church considered that a day started at sunset, so the evening before All Hallows was part of the same day, in church-speak. The evening of October 31 and the daylight hours of November 1 were the same day and the church kept a special vigil in the evening. Of course, that's where the name comes from. 'All Hallows Evening' was shortened to Hallowe'en.

And so the two traditions, pagan and Christian, carried on, twined uneasily together. Candles in turnip 'lanterns' came in, Jack-o-lanterns, after a folk tale about a farmer called Stingy Jack who tricked the devil, and in return had to wander the earth at night for ever with only a candle in a hollowed out turnip. In the nineteenth century these traditions were taken across the water to North America by Irish and Scottish settlers, where they flourished and grew, coming back to us elaborated by pumpkins (easier to carve than turnips) and by Hollywood images from horror films.

The Children's Society has a website about all this (www.halloweenchoice.org). They believe that Halloween has the power to trivialise evil and can be portrayed as celebrating the triumph of evil over good – when in fact Christians hold that the opposite is true and that, in Christ, good conquers evil. They are concerned that Halloween activities build an excessive fear of evil in children, and a negative sense of their own vulnerability in a dangerous and dark world. They admit that Christians have a wide range of views on what they mean by 'the devil', but say that the one thing they all agree on is that the reality of evil needs to be taken very seriously. Whether 'the devil' is seen as a personal being or a symbol of evil is less important. What matters is to fight against evil, whatever form it comes in. The danger with Halloween is that it suggests it is evil that wins.

In recent years attempts have been made to provide alternative forms of Halloween. Some churches have suggested children's festivals of light, with everyone dressing up in costumes representing their heroes. I guess little ones might go for it, but it's hard to see the older ones resisting peer-pressure and going along to church that night dressed as Mother Theresa or a fireman. It's all too artificial, too imposed.

And because Halloween is so commercialised now it's difficult to see how the shops might turn around and promote more positive interpretations. On the other hand, as someone has said, few people would have imagined, a decade or so ago that organic food would be taken up so widely and sold alongside the non-organic in ordinary shops. If we could find a good new aspect of Halloween might not the shops sell it alongside the horror stuff, so that parents and children could choose?

If we go back to its origins can we usefully bring them into the twenty-first century? I'm thinking for a start about that 'thin' time that they felt centuries ago. The turning point between autumn and winter, when the boundary between the living and the dead seemed less solid. Most of us have lost that sense, lost the intuition of it. But it must be a very basic human sense because it exists in so many different cultures. Somewhere within us that sense must be still touch-able. Those days at the end of October and the beginning of November could be a time when we really remember our ancestors, perhaps going in great numbers (with lanterns!) to decorate their graves on All Hallows Eve, celebrating the great ones on All Saints day, and remembering all of them, good or bad, on All Souls day. Somewhere during that time we might introduce a twenty-first century contribution, an acknowledgement that some of our 'ghosts' have done us harm, which we need to acknowledge in order to set out on the path of forgiveness – for our own spiritual health and well-being.

They say that in old times children had salt sprinkled on their heads to ward off evil at Halloween. That sounds good, a ritual of God's protection. We could do that again. We could keep the pumpkin lanterns: they can have smiling faces. And when we light them we can tell the story of Stingy Jack, because what it says is that messing with evil is asking for serious trouble. There could be wonderful church services with dramatic plunges into darkness and then candles and then into full light, followed by prayers and wishes being cast into bonfires, and parties with apple-bobbing, and mountains of barmbrack.

This may not be it, but there must be a better way than the rubbish event we have now.

24

A Chance to Be a Happier and Healthier Society

The author hopes that the economic downturn might give us the opportunity to rediscover the real treasures of life, such as community, friendship and trust
[1 November 2008]

Sometimes when tragedy strikes a family that is when it discovers that the things that really matter are not possessions but other people, and relationships. What good is a grand house and a yacht and big money in the bank if there are no others to love and be loved by? What good is gaining the whole world if you lose your heart and your soul?

Times like the present, if not tragic, can be frightening. For the people whose business income is going down, and for the men and women who are in danger of losing their jobs. And especially for those who have already lost them. Anxious times for everyone affected in so many different ways by the general turn-down in the economy and the government's attempts to shore it up.

But if there is a silver lining to this dark cloud it seems to be that we've reached a turning point. Not one we would have chosen, but – like nasty medicine – one that might in the end make us a happier, healthier, and altogether nicer society. Don't we all know, deep down, that the rapid up-surge of wealth in this country has spoiled so much that we value? At first the Celtic tiger was beautiful, making up for the centuries of poverty and oppression. A recompense, almost, for surviving them. But didn't it then gradually go sour, with the demands of the newly rich forcing up the cost of basics, making the poor even poorer? Wasn't there a sense that, flooded with glitz and bling, Ireland of the Welcomes was becoming Ireland of the Go-aways and Get-losts?

Maybe as it all begins to come tumbling down we are getting a chance to save ourselves. Maybe as we see that money is only money we will rediscover the real treasures of life. Rediscover words like community, friendship, trust. Rediscover that a picnic can give as much delight as a ludicrously expensive meal in an over-decorated restaurant. That joining a choir or a writing group costs next to nothing but brings you new friends and a huge sense of creativity. That a child can do more with a cardboard box than with a toy that costs a fortune and is discarded in boredom. That buying clothes from a charity shop not only gives scope to the imagination but also a modest buzz from knowing help is being given to people who really need help.

Something similar is surely happening at a spiritual level. Religion has been in obvious decline in Ireland for a number of decades. If we stand back from it and look carefully the reasons are fairly clear. It has been too much led from the top, too much along authority-lines that worked a century or two ago but don't work now. That authority dried up our spirituality. Now we are finding it for ourselves, swimming out into deeper seas and leaving the authority figures stranded on rocks of immobility.

Survey after survey shows that yes, people are religious, they are spiritual, but they don't go to church very much any more because 'church' doesn't feed their souls. They look for food in other places: in music and pictures and books and films, in other forms of religion like Buddhism, or new forms that are experimental and unorganised. A Europe-wide survey of 21,000 people this year found that 27% did not belong to any church, yet 74% considered themselves religious.

At the same time, piece after piece of research is showing the benefits of 'good' religion. Here are just a few:

Faith can combat physical pain. This month's issue of the medical journal, *Pain*, reported on a study in which regular mass-goers were tested alongside atheists and agnostics. Each one was shown a religious picture while being given minor electric shocks to the hand. The people with religious faith experienced measurably less pain because, they said, they felt calm and had a sense of being 'taken care of'.

Religious belief makes people more trusting, honest and generous than they would otherwise be. News of this piece of research came from *Science* magazine a couple of weeks ago. It seems to be saying that when we believe in God we do what is good and right because we have a feeling of being observed. That's not exactly flattering but it's difficult to disagree with it.

Many serious scholars are claiming that human rights, social democracy and freedom of conscience spring from Judeo-Christian thinking, and that its understanding of humanity and the world and God is basic to social good.

But perhaps the most significant new thinking is about worship. At its best, worship lifts the heart, gives courage and strength, and builds community. It includes singing (which does all sorts of good things for us) and – ideally – silence. More and more we are being told that we need stillness and silence in our lives. The Archbishop of Canterbury, in an interview in the Muslim magazine *Emel*, said, 'There is something about western modernity which really does eat away at the soul.' He was saying that the modern way of life turns people into things. We are identified by what we do. And we do too much. We need to give more time to just being, through activities like art, prayer, holidays. Not with any purpose but like children at play. Psychologist Mihály Czíkszentmihályi claims that it is in times of quiet, focused absorption that we are happiest. Remember what used to be called 'companionable silence'? That state when people are quietly reading or sewing or whatever, aware of other people around them but without needing to talk? It used to be one of the joys of a public library. It also happens if you are at a retreat house where meals are eaten in silence yet you remain alert to someone needing you to pass the salt. Somehow, communal silence nourishes us.

So perhaps, in the end, this economic crisis will be good for us. As an old hymn says, 'the clouds you so much dread ... will break in blessings on your head.' I guess it's up to us to let it bless us.

25

Twelve Days but No Partridge in a Pear Tree

The author wonders if there's a way of blending the commercial and religious ways of preparing for Christmas [15 November 2008]

The first signs of Christmas appeared in some of our shops in October. Now, although it's only mid-November, they are gearing up for the glittering seduction of our purses, and the final full-blooded attack on our wallets. Do you love it? Or hate it? For most of us, probably, the answer is, both.

But maybe this is a good time for a quiet think about what it all means. It would be good to say that even if the world has got Christmas all twisted, the churches have got it right. It was, after all, theirs to start with. But they seem to have lost the advantage. Christmas in the churches seems to be out of step with real life. As a bishop once said, 'For the Church, Christmas *begins* on December 25, for the world of commerce it ends the day before.'

The Church wants us to observe Advent all through December, a time of sober prayer and spiritual preparation, of anticipation, building up to the glory that will burst upon us when we celebrate the birth of the Christ-child on the 25th. In the old days it was even a time of fasting. Now I know some will say that it's us who are out of step with our churches, that we should be observing Advent in a serious manner. And maybe if we were all monks and nuns we would, but we're not. It just doesn't work. All through December the great majority of us are doing the very opposite of fasting, and our preparations are so frantically practical they leave little room for anything spiritual. The parties and the carols start a long time before the 25th, and mince pies are obligatory at every function that takes place in December. It's really as if the first Sunday of Advent (November 30 this year) is the signal to start making whoopee.

I guess we can't turn the clock back. When I was a kid tangerines (clementines, satsumas, whatever) were only available in the winter. Santa always left a tangerine in the toe of our Christmas stocking. Although they were on sale for a few weeks before the big day, none of us ever had one before that magically scented one was peeled out of our stocking in the dark stillness of our Christmas morning awakening. So I was appalled when I got married and found that my husband would eat tangerines as soon as they arrived in the shops. How self-indulgent, I thought. How undisciplined. I tried to persuade him that he was missing out on the ecstatic pleasure of waiting and then getting, but he wasn't to be persuaded. Nor can we all be persuaded, now, to observe a time of fasting and hair-shirt-wearing from November 30 to December 25.

Is there any way we can blend together the two ways, religious and commercial, of preparing for Christmas? Some people have suggested that Advent should be in November but that seems like a non-starter. There have been churches that have tried to hold back the tide by having no tree or crib until Christmas Eve, and no carols before Christmas Day. The trouble with that is that after the Day the church tends to shut down and take a holiday. By the following week it's New Year and carols seem hopelessly out of place.

Some people would like to see the Twelve Days of Christmas come back. Not for giving each other those impractical partridges in pear-trees, but to spread the festivities from one day to twelve. It's a nice idea. Instead of gradually getting into the carols and mince pies as December progresses, you save them for a clear-cut start on Christmas Day and then have nearly two weeks of them. Right through to Little Christmas, the day of the coming of the Three Kings (the Epiphany) on January 6. For twelve long days there'd be a feast of carol services and carol singing for charities, parties, nativity plays and social gatherings. The giving of presents could be spread out over the days. It would be a great time for a *scoraíocht* and lots of those long healthy walks that at present most of us only do on St Stephen's Day. And of course there'd be mince pies every day (surely the Twelve Days is the basis of the superstition that you have to eat twelve to have a good year) and all the other special-season foods. But they could be laid out over the whole holiday instead of having to be consumed all on one bloated day.

Some old cookery books give recipes for something called Twelfth Night cake. Because of the ancient method of counting a day from sunset to sunset, Twelfth Night is January 5, the eve of Twelfth Day, January 6. So you begin the holiday with Christmas cake and end it, as you take the decorations down, with Twelfth Night cake. (Ah, but Lent will be a short way ahead, when you can fast and take all the weight off again.)

It would be easy, of course, for the spiritual side of Christmas to get lost in all this. But it doesn't have to. What Christmas is really about is recognising that God is not apart from the world but is present in it. Jesus is the sign of that divine presence among us, and by celebrating his birth we are acknowledging that God is in the world, and helping to make that more apparent. Call that presence the Kingdom of God if you want to, or the Kingdom of Heaven. Some now prefer to call it the Republic of God. Whichever phrase you use, Jesus famously told his followers that it was coming, but also that it was already present within them.

The best way we can build that state of heaven is in community with the people around us, with family and friends and neighbours and strangers, especially with those who are in any sort of need. Celebrating Christmas, when it is more concerned with giving ourselves than with spending big money, is surely celebrating community, and must delight the heart of God.

26

Christmas Past ... and Present and Future Too

The author believes that Christmas, through its traditions and rituals, inevitably transports us back to Christmases past – yet Christmas must also be our way forward into the future [20 December 2008]

'No ham for Christmas?' The possibility of being deprived of that traditional food was an interesting sidelight to the recent withdrawal of pork products. Ham goes with turkey, and for most of us the two together make up our Christmas dinners.

For Christmas to be Christmas we require a lot of traditional things. A young American Jewish friend, spending her first winter away from home, asked us why our Christmas foods were all the same. She was puzzled why the Christmas pudding and the Christmas cake and the mince pies were 'all made of the same ingredients' – basically dried fruit and sugar. We did of course give her the answer in terms of history, that in centuries past this was a way of preserving summer foods for winter eating. But the real answer was simply that these things are now traditional. No matter how much the posh magazines devise alternative menus and recipes, most us want the foods that belong to the season. They are what we've always had, or tried to have, every year.

There is surely no time of year more likely to bring up the past than Christmas. Because there is so much tradition wrapped into it, everything we do can remind us of how we did it ten, twenty or more years ago. When we decorate the tree the baubles that have been put away year after year bring back a cluster of memories of other times and other places. Going into church on Christmas Eve or Christmas morning you are liable to be overcome by a re-visitation of your childhood, of a time when you held your breath in awe and wonder. And I know that when I'm standing at the kitchen table this Christmas Eve, rolling out the pastry for the mince pies while listening to the very best of the carols on the radio, I'll be back again in another kitchen of long ago, surrounded by small children, with my mother-in-law rocking the baby while I make the pies, and those same carols hushing and swelling above the chatter of the young ones. My mother-in-law has been dead for many years now, but she's always there on Christmas Eve.

Whether all the memories make us happy or sad, it seems we can't escape them at this time. The past is very much a part of Christmas. And that's part of the value of traditional rituals. But there has to be more than that. The Christmas story is not set only in the past.

Two thousand years ago there was born in the Middle East a Jewish baby who grew up to change the history of the world. He left his family and became a wandering preacher, and his teaching was fresh and marvellous. After his death his followers called him the Christ, meaning 'the anointed one', and eventually broke away from Judaism and called themselves Christians.

As the world grew, the celebration of the birth of this Jesus was in many countries added on to the celebration of the winter solstice which turns us towards spring. We don't know what time of year Jesus was really born, and it doesn't matter. That birth, and all that it means, fits perfectly with the winter solstice. It's all about moving from darkness to light, and human beings have always known the life-giving importance of that. The beautiful book of Isaiah in the Hebrew scriptures says:

'The people who walked in darkness
have seen a great light;
those who dwelt in a land of deep darkness,
upon them the light has dawned.'

And the first chapter of the Gospel of Luke contains these lines:

In the tender compassion of our God
    the dawn from on high shall break upon us,
    to shine on those who dwell in darkness
    and the shadow of death
    and to guide our feet into the way of peace.

For Christians, this is the meaning of Christmas. Remembering the birth of Jesus, and from that to his life through to his death, says to us that even when we are in utter darkness there is light ahead for us. Everything that Jesus was about can be summed up in that one brief description that he gave when he was asked what a person should do: 'Love God, and love your neighbour.' And love, above all else, is what dispels the darkness.

Sometimes it's the love that we give to God that does it, sometimes it's the loving-kindness that we feel coming from God. Sometimes it's the love we receive from other human beings, our 'neighbours', that brings us out of darkness, but it can also happen when we ourselves show loving-kindness to others.

Another way of saying all this is: God is with us. 'God-with-us' is the meaning of the word 'Emmanuel'. In the book of Isaiah 'Emmanuel' is used in some places to mean the land of Palestine and in other places it is the name of a person, a specific messiah figure. There's no conflict there. The word can be applied to a place and to a person also. In the Gospel of Matthew we hear that Mary is told that her baby will be called Jesus, and Emmanuel. No conflict there either. Jesus will be an Emmanuel figure. He won't just talk about God, he will be a walking talking sign of God-with-us.

He still is that sign. Jesus was not just someone who lived and died centuries ago. Christmas is a celebration that the spirit of that man is still at work among us, influencing us, strengthening us, bringing light out of our darkness. It's a celebration of his presence.

So Christmas is not just about the past. If we are to get the best of it, it must be about our way forward into the future. Not just re-telling the wonderland story of angels and stars and snow and kings with gifts that we have been telling for 2000 years. But grasping, by whatever means, the strange concept that the spirit of that wandering preacher is still available to us, can live within us and within our communities, can change our lives and then change our world.

27

Thorniest Item on the Agenda of Ecumenism

The author explains that for most Christians the
Eucharist is the most basic and most essential part
of their religion [31 January 2009]

Some of us call it the Mass, some call it Holy Communion, some call it the Lord's Supper. The name that is used when Christians of different sorts get together to talk about it is the Eucharist, which comes from a Greek word meaning 'thanksgiving', itself a translation of the Hebrew word *beraka* or 'blessing'.

For most Christians the Eucharist is the most basic and most essential part of our religion. But we don't only have different names for it, we have different ideas about what it means. For some this blessing, this giving thanks, is simply a 'memorial' or remembering of the Last Supper that Jesus had with his disciples before his death, when, in the traditional Jewish manner, he blessed the bread and wine they were about to consume. For others, it is something so mysterious, so holy, that when we receive the bread and the wine we receive the very presence of Christ. Between those two extremes there would be a great many variations in the way we think about it.

And because we have different ideas, some of our churches say we can't take a full part in each others' Eucharists. A Protestant, for example, can be present at a Catholic Mass, but can't receive communion, the bread and the wine. Catholics are not allowed by their church to receive communion in anything but a Catholic church.

The people at the top of our churches say we must have full agreement and integration before we can share this sacrament. More and more ground-level Christians are becoming impatient with this shutting-out of each other.

The other issue that sometimes attracts radical thinking is the question of who should preside at the Eucharist. Does it have to be an ordained person, or can a lay person do it? If a layperson could do it would they still have to be somehow authorised by their church? This question comes up at the 'high' and the 'low' ends of Christianity. It comes up when Catholics in remote areas of South America can only hear Mass once a month or less because their priest must travel for hundreds of miles to get to them. So, if there aren't enough priests, the thinking goes, shouldn't a lay person be chosen by each community to celebrate the Mass for them? Isn't it more important that they should receive communion weekly, than that they should only receive it from a priest?

This question also comes up where there is quite a 'low' view of priesthood and the sacraments, such as one part of the Anglican church in Australia where they battled for years for 'lay presidency'.

There's another way it comes up. When prayer groups or bible-study groups or religious communities meet together regularly they sometimes have a time of worship that includes a simple sharing of bread and wine in the Lord's name. Even when there is no ordained person present. What is this if it not a Eucharist? If, as I believe, this is happening quietly but increasingly often, it may turn out to be the way forward, cutting through the territory-guarding over-cautiousness of the church hierarchies.

Last week a group of Christians of many denominations and traditions met together in Drogheda to talk about all this. This was the 44th Greenhills Ecumenical Conference, and the theme was, 'The Eucharist: Yesterday, Today and Tomorrow'.

The main speaker was the Revd Professor Brendan Leahy, a Roman Catholic priest in the Archdiocese of Dublin and Professor of Systematic Theology at St Patrick's College, Maynooth. Responding speakers were Lindsay Hall, a Methodist lay preacher and on the staff of the Church of Ireland Theological College in Dublin, and Grace Clunie, a priest in the Church of Ireland and Director of Celtic Spirituality at Armagh Cathedral.

I guess you wouldn't expect anything too radical from a Catholic professor at Maynooth, especially when Archbishop Seán Brady was in the audience to hear him. Professor Leahy led us through a mini-history of the thinking of the Catholic church and the Reformed churches on the Eucharist. He quoted St Paul saying, 'Because there is one bread, we who are many are one body, for we all partake of the one bread.' He quoted Martin Luther saying that access to the Mass is not by our works or our merits but by faith alone. He spoke about the International Methodist-Catholic Dialogue Commission and its 2006 report which said that areas for further dialogue included 'the nature and validity of the ministry of those who preside at the Eucharist, the precise meaning of the Eucharist, [and] the particular way in which Christ is present in Holy Communion'. But in the end he re-stated that we cannot yet share the Eucharist with other Christians, and recommended patience.

The two women speakers, I suspect, are less patient. Lindsay Hall declared the Eucharist to be the thorniest item on the agenda of ecumenism. How can we share the Eucharist with people whose doctrine of the Eucharist is different? Yet even within our own denominations, she said, it is unlikely that everyone has the same understanding of what is happening. And if we don't share, we are denying ourselves a great gift. Our coming together is more likely to happen through the very act of sharing the Eucharist. We are not called to resolve all the problems before we move, she said. Christ will do that.

Grace Clunie spoke of chapter two of the Acts of the Apostles, where the followers of Jesus met together regularly, after his death, breaking bread together and eating their food 'with glad and generous hearts, praising God'. Clearly this was the beginnings of the Eucharist, but no mention of priests. But the church has clericalised the Eucharist so much that Acts 2 is hardly recognisable. There is pain in all this. 'When the validity of your ministry is questioned, when you're turned away from the sacramental meal, or told that you cannot participate, there's pain in that experience,' she said. Yet what God offers us in this sacrament is hospitality, gentle hospitality. Her closing words still echo in my head: 'Because he is the host, not us.'

I was reminded of an Anglican Communion service where everyone present was invited to receive, no questions asked, 'because it is the Lord's table, not ours'. And I wondered, how can we ever say, in his name, that some may come to it and some may not?

28

Give Up 'Giving Up' if it Makes Others Miserable

The author considers the tradition of 'giving up for Lent' and asks friends about the different ways they choose to observe this custom, which in modern times has come to be seen as more of a choice than an obligation
[14 February 2009]

Do you give up sugar for Lent? Or alcohol? Meat? Cigarettes? (And give what you save to charity?) It's an odd thing, this 'giving up for Lent'. What's it for? And how many still do it? I've been asking friends.

But I began by reading John Henry Newman, later Cardinal Newman, and maybe one day Saint John Henry Newman. This is what he wrote in his diary in 1842, three years before he moved from the Church of England to the Roman Catholic Church:

'I have not been quite so strict this Lent as last. I have been stricter in one point, that I have eaten nothing between breakfast (8am) and tea (6pm), and in not eating even fish – but I have relaxed, in having tea and butter and hot milk... I did not dine out, I did not wear gloves – I eat rhubarb commonly with my butter. I have not seen the Oxford or London papers except once.'

'Giving up' is all based on the story of Jesus fasting for 40 days in the wilderness before beginning his public ministry. Lent is 40 days of preparation for Easter, a time for soul-searching and repentance. It's like the Jewish Yom Kippur, ending the Ten Days of Repentance when Jews try to amend their behaviour and seek forgiveness for wrongs done against God and against other people.

In Christianity's early centuries people fasted two or three days each week. That meant having only one meal a day, in the evening. So it's also like Ramadan, the month-long period of fasting that Muslims still observe every year.

Christians were expected to abstain from eating meat, eggs and dairy produce. That's why we have pancakes the day before Lent begins, to use up all the eggs. And why we have eggs at Easter, to celebrate the end of the fast.

Festivities were not allowed in Lent (we still have no marriages in church then), and people gave work or money to charity, and more time than usual to religious devotions. After the Church split into Catholic and Protestant these practices continued. But the fasting gradually faded to simply eating fish instead of meat, on two days a week, and even that practice has diminished.

So what's the point of all that? And do people still do it at all? I asked some friends: four Anglicans, three Catholics and one Protestant, though not in that order. I've changed their names.

Helen: 'I once gave up chocolate for Lent. I thought about it every day and decided this had not helped me spiritually at all. I gave up giving things up. What I do now is to try to address one particular thing that needs attention. This may be a person, or a study topic, or it may be an increasingly bad habit that needs checking.'

Joanne: 'As a Catholic child I gave up sweets every Lent – although I used to save any I was given to eat after Easter! In my twenties I felt that many of the Catholic Church's teachings were contrary to the Bible, not least doctrines on penance and the basis of our personal salvation.' (She quotes the letter of Paul to the Romans: God 'justifies the one who has faith in Jesus'.) 'Now I would rather rejoice and thank God for His many blessings and good things He has given me to enjoy. That is not to say that self-discipline is a bad thing. But I think it better to direct it at positive action – and not to confine it to Lent.'

Stephen: 'Last Lent I tried giving up worrying – asked Jesus to help carry my burdens and let me rest a bit, to 'restore my soul'. I'm still here, and feisty, so I may well do the same again this year! Worry is dysfunctional, an anticipation of things we fear and have no control over.'

Nell: 'Adding something seems more meaningful than giving something up. This Lent I'll be trying to establish a practice of reading Morning and Evening prayer. I do this sporadically, but I'd like it to become routine rather than optional.

Taigdh and Teresa: 'Regarding Lent we do not 'give up' as such. Lent for us is 40 days of focusing on Gethsemane, Calvary and the Resurrection ... the suffering and the glory ... by our ministry of singing. It is, for us, a time to focus on leading a true Christian Life ... preaching the gospel by example ... using words only when necessary. We have been blessed so much in our lives that Lent is a time of gratitude and re-commitment to the principles of our Christian faith.'

Luke: 'I am all for fasting in Lent (and all the other days prescribed by the Book of Common Prayer). As a species we are designed for periods when the food is plentiful and for periods of famine, and our bodies work better under these conditions, but we do not like them! So I think that it is a healthy discipline to fast at regular intervals.

What do I mean by fasting? I mean eating less than we would usually eat, and for me that means having only one meal of solid food per day, and that meal no larger that the one that I would normally eat for lunch or dinner.

I also abide by the direction of Jesus, that when I fast, I try to do it in secret. If we are invited out to dinner during

Lent I will go, and eat what is provided, and counterbalance it by fasting extra another time.

What good does this do to me spiritually? Well, I think it instils some discipline into me, and helps me to control my desires in all sorts of spheres. When I am very hungry, and desperate to eat, I use the Jesus Prayer, and I think that this helps me to understand Jesus better. I know this sounds very weak, but for me it is very strong.'

Roberta: 'I rather like Lent and I do try to 'give up' something. Coffee would be a really big thing for me. So that will be a beginning.'

There are other possibilities. Eco-Congregation Ireland hope that people will set up an environmental study group in their parish for Lent, or plant a tree, or cut down their carbon use, perhaps by using public transport instead of their car. Christian Aid is running a Lenten 'Journey to Jerusalem' on the internet, a virtual pilgrimage into the heart of Israel-Palestine using short videos, podcasts, photo galleries, prayers and stories.

Not all giving up is good. A friend of a friend was at an audience with Pope John XXIII some time close to the beginning of Lent. The pope pointed jovially to his secretary and said: 'If he gives up smoking again this year he'll be getting grumpy and making everybody else miserable, as he did last year. So I'm instructing him to give up making everybody miserable instead!'

29

Passing a Camel through the Eye of a Needle

The author believes that we must clarify what is literally true in our creeds and scriptures and what is simply an imaginative way of saying something [7 March 2009]

'She was literally up to her neck in bills,' someone said on the radio recently. You could see what the speaker meant. He was wanting to stress how very many bills the unfortunate woman had received. But 'literally'? No, she didn't really have bits of paper piling up around her to neck-level. Just as it never *literally* rains cats and dogs, or we'd have dead and wounded animals all over the streets. 'Literally' means 'exactly what it says'. 'Up to her neck in bills' is not literal. It's a metaphor, a brought-in image that gives you an idea of how extreme the situation was.

I've just been reading a book about the Bible that is all about the dangers of taking things literally.* The author thinks that a huge amount of damage has been done to Christianity by well-meaning Christians who have taken too much of it too literally. We've failed to appreciate that in the times when the Bible was being written people were accustomed to speaking in metaphors. When Jesus said that it was

---

* James Rowe Adams: *From Literal to Literary: The Essential Reference Book for Biblical Metaphors* (Pilgrim Press, 2005-2008)

harder for a rich man to get to heaven than for a camel to pass through the eye of a needle, he didn't mean that people were in the habit of trying to thread camels through needles. It was a metaphor, an image of just how impossible it was. Unfortunately, some Bible commentaries have tried to find reasons to take it literally, like maybe there was a monument called the Needle, with a low doorway that it was difficult to get camels through. They just couldn't allow it be a metaphor.

Jesus spoke in parables, a form of metaphor. 'A landowner planted a vineyard...' 'A woman lost a coin...' No-one thought he was talking about real flesh-and-blood people, they knew it was a story, and that the story was told to make a point. Most people hearing those stories now know they're not literally true. But what about when Jesus calls God 'Father'? Is God literally his father, or is it just a helpful image? What about the story of Jesus's birth that was written down generations later, a story that includes a virgin birth, and angels and visiting wise men? Could those be metaphors? What about a body risen from the dead? Is that a metaphor? Increasing numbers of Christians say Yes to these questions. And their faith does not melt away when they allow themselves say it. Instead, it can be a huge relief and the beginning of new spiritual growth.

Some of the metaphors in the Bible are very important indeed, especially when they concern God. We refer to God as 'he'. Therefore the majority of people visualise God – whether they believe in God or not – as a male person. We know in our heads that is a metaphor, because God is not a human person. But at heart-level and gut-level we do believe that is what God is. It doesn't help that our language has no word for a being you can relate to, except for 'she' and 'he'. It doesn't help that the Bible has added on to God words like 'father', 'king', 'lord', or even 'shepherd'. They all reinforce an image of a kindly (or tyrannical) male. And it doesn't help that for some centuries the Church has talked about 'three *persons* in one God'. There's a Father, and a Son, and a vague figure called the Holy Spirit. If you query that you'll be told that it doesn't really mean three people, in the human sense. There is no way we should take it literally. Yet once again what we picture (three people) conflicts with what we are supposed to know in our heads (*not* three people).

The problem is that different people look at religion in different ways.

Early in the twentieth century the Roman Catholic writer Baron Friedrich von Hügel outlined three elements of religious and spiritual growth. The first, he said, is institutional, as when children get to know the traditions and creeds of religion, soaking them up without any questions or objections. The second is the intellectual phase, usually begun in adolescence, when young people want to make sense of it all for themselves. Many fail to do so, and drop out at this stage. But if they stay and grow they move into the third stage, which is intuitive or mystical. Without abandoning the institution or their intellect they are able to live without hard and fast answers, but with an awareness of the sacred and with trust in the unknown.

The first stage expects everything to be literal. The third stage is comfortable with metaphor. The second stage, the intellectually exploring stage, is where we move from one to the other.

Our churches do not have a great record of the sort of teaching that would help us to move. More and more people, who haven't been encouraged to move even beyond the first stage, much less the second, are looking at what they think is Christianity and saying, quite rightly, 'I can't believe all that.' So the number of self-declared atheists is on the rise. The tragedy is that so many men and women think they are required to believe 'all that'. Often their atheism is a simple rejection of those literal ideas and images that literalist Christians have been telling them was the only real thing.

If we have any hope of Christianity surviving this century we must help each other to move into the third stage, where faith leaves behind the insecure demand for certainty through Biblical literalism, and opens out into large horizons. And to make that moving possible it would surely help if we could clarify what is literally true in our creeds and scriptures, and what is simply an imaginative way of saying something. It would take courage, but is surely better than letting Christianity die.

30

Not Right When Rich Get Richer and Poor Get Poorer

The author talks to Rector Paul Draper about the
disparity between Angola's wealth and the extreme
poverty of the ordinary people [28 March 2009]

Under an African sun, in a building with a corrugated roof but no walls, the church service went on for two hours. But Paul Draper from West Cork was not bored. 'I didn't want it to stop,' he says. 'I was thinking, "These people have got it." Here in Ireland we worry about buildings and finances. They have none of that. But they are rich in quality relationships. They make the church beautiful with lengths of fabric. Everyone is involved, from the young to the old.'

As Rector of Ballydehob, Paul had built up good contacts with the charity Christian Aid. One year, when the Southwest Co-ordinator, Andrew Coleman, did a Harvest Thanksgiving service for the parishioners he gave them a challenge. He asked them to help rebuild a school that had been wrecked in Angola's seven-year civil war, which ended in 2002.

Christian Aid works closely with its partners in many countries, and staff go regularly to evaluate the work, especially in three areas: HIV/Aids education and care, accountable governance, and sustainable livelihoods of the people. In 2008 the charity's Head of Development was due to go to Angola for two weeks with the Communications Officer and a member of the Christian Aid board, and they wanted to complete the team with a supporter. Because of Ballydehob's connection with the country, the Rector was an obvious choice.

'When I was asked to go, it was a big thing for me. A wonderful opportunity. But so far outside my own comfort zone, I had no idea what to expect.' He had some serious training: lots of briefings and a full day in Dublin. It was all very practical, including basic Portuguese – and what to do if kidnapped.

His first impression, when the plane touched down at Luanda, was of noise and movement. It is a city of huge contrasts, with big modern buildings on the seafront, and round behind them acres of slums of makeshift housing with no sanitation. The disparity, he says, was 'head-wrecking'.

From 1961 to 1974 Angola fought for its independence from Portugal. That was followed by the civil war, 1975-2002, totalling nearly 40 years of fighting. The landscape is still littered with collapsed bridges, abandoned tanks. There are landmines: Angola is the most land-mined country in the world. Some areas are cleared of mines, but it is still necessary to know where it is safe to go.

After 24 hours in Luanda the group flew again, down the coast for three days in two other cities, and then into the centre of the country. They met the team which had overseen the rebuilding of the school that Ballydehob had supported. They sat in on an after-school meeting, where training facilities and counselling are supported by Christian Aid. Here girls learn computer skills, cookery, sewing, life choices, and get education on HIV – how to prevent it, how to treat it, how it affects families. From these courses the girls gain self-confidence. They know they could be infected, but they choose not to be. And they pass that news on to their friends, too.

'These girls are a real beacon of hope for Angola,' Paul says. 'They talked with confidence, in a room full of friends and complete strangers, about intercourse and how to avoid infection. Some of them visit people who are already infected, providing simple counselling, telling them, "It's not a life sentence." Most of them want to put something back into the community when they are older.'

In another area the visitors met members of Umonga, an organisation which reunites families who were separated by the civil war. Those whose families cannot be found are still living in tents. Paul was shocked at their domestic conditions, but also at how positive and happy they were.

'That was a very happy day,' he says. 'A new baby had been born, and they took us to see him. They named him Jesus.'

'Another day we were invited to a village meeting. The men sat in circles in the centre, the women in an outer circle. I kept wanting to offer my seat to them but I was told I couldn't do that. The meeting ended early because there had been a death in the locality and people needed to go and visit the family. There are so many deaths there, of people in their 30s and 40s. They live so far from any health care. Life expectancy is 40 for men, 43 for women, and one in four children die before they are five.'

Christian Aid's Angolan manager, Rosario, arranged for the visitors to meet a succession of interesting people at meal times. These included a Roman Catholic priest with a degree in Justice and Peace, and Pastor Luis, of the Congregational Church. Luis and his brother were separated in the civil war and found later that they had been fighting on opposite sides. Their reunion is a symbol of hope for the country.

It was at Luis's church that Paul experienced the beautiful two hour long service, and where he was impressed by the amount of lay involvement. 'There was a choir of 20 to 30 young people, plus a male choir, plus the regular church choir.' He was also impressed by Pastor Luis's sermon. 'It was a really astute sermon, about the coming election, covering all the key areas, all the issues.'

'My over-riding feeling, seeing the increasing development in Angola plus the untold amount of poverty, is wondering why they can't join it up. People don't seem overly angry with the government. They are grateful for anything, but not at all critical. If anyone does speak out, they will be co-opted by the more astute politicians. But if they are too vocal they will be shut out. Yet it is part of growing a civil society that you can allow the voice of criticism.'

Inevitably, Paul compares what he has seen in Angola with the way we live here. 'It's not right if a country gets richer and the poverty of ordinary people increases. It's a cliché, but I re-evaluated everything when I came back. When I got off the plane at Cork airport the first thing I saw was all the billboards, promoting consumer goods. I felt physically sick.'

In June, Paul and his wife Kathryn and their two daughters leave for the deanery of Lismore. Parishioners there will be blessed, as Ballydehob has been for fifteen years, by his spirituality, concern and compassion, surely deepened by his visit to Angola.

31

In Touch with Something Greater than Ourselves

The question of whether atheists pray leads the author to ask if it is hard-wired into human beings to 'pray' to 'something greater than themselves' [11 April 2009]

Some friends and I have been having a great correspondence by email – about prayer. It seems to have started when one of them wondered if atheists pray. About half the group thought the question was a non-starter. No God, no praying. Some of the others said they believed that everyone prays, in the sense of calling on something greater than themselves, especially in emergencies. There's some evidence that it's hard-wired into human beings. Maybe an atheist has to actively fight against an impulse to pray?

Then, in our conversations, it came down to, 'It depends what you mean by prayer, and it depends what you mean by God.' You can't connect with 'God' without some idea of what it is you are relating to. And that 'God' can be the straight-down-the-line one that most of us learnt about from the Catechism or Sunday School. A God who is male and elderly and who has spoken to us in the Bible. At the other extreme, it can be a universal spirit that we sense but know nothing factual about. Probably for most of us God is some- where between those two. That's a wide range.

If that's wide, so is the idea of prayer. According to the dictionary, prayer is 'a solemn and humble request to God, or to an object of worship; a supplication, a petition, or thanksgiving, usually expressed in words.' But then, what do dictionaries know? That definition is so limited. Apart from the word 'thanksgiving' it's entirely about asking. Sadly, that's all a lot of people think prayer is. Asking. 'Please let her get well.' 'Please let me pass my Leaving.' 'Let me win the Lotto!!' Or simply, 'Help!'

I know two people whose friendship was nearly ended when one of them felt driven to say, 'You only get in touch when you want something.' If our relationship with God dries up maybe it's because we've only been in touch when we wanted something. Our church services don't help much here. Apart from 'saying sorry' for the ways we've failed to be the wonderful people we were created to be, our church prayers are all 'asking' prayers. And they are all prayers of words out of our heads.

Formal praying is a head-thing. Personal praying comes more from what the old translations of the Bible sometimes

called 'the reins'. 'God searcheth the hearts and the reins,' it
says in Psalm 7 verse 9. It meant the kidneys. That's where
the ancient Hebrews thought that all our knowledge and joy
and pain and pleasure lived. We might say that formal praying comes from our heads but real prayer comes from our
guts.

The good news is that more and more church services
contain periods of wordlessness. Periods of silence, in which
ideally we rest in a wordless sense of being in the presence
of the divine. A sort of mini-meditation time.

Meditation is for many of us the best form of prayer altogether. No asking, no words at all, no images or pictures,
no thinking at all. A simple existing in the present moment
allows into us an awareness of being part of something much
greater than ourselves, something nurturing, something of
pure goodness and a quiet joy.

Now what happens if an atheist meditates? I have to admit I don't know any who do, but they surely could if meditation is understood in the way it is often promoted in the
media, as a way to calm your mind and body and so achieve
better mental and physical health. No God-stuff there. Yet I
can't think that anyone could meditate and not in the end be
in touch with that sense of something greater.

One of the people in our email conversation about
prayer sits very lightly to organised religion. Yet she said she
regrets that many people are taking up the practice of meditation 'without a road map'. She feels that a framework is
needed to make sense of all that comes up when you meditate, and she wishes the churches were providing it. What
churchgoers hear from the pulpit or the altar has little con-

nection, she said, with the 'popular spirituality' which is so much on the increase.

The days of the iron-handed authority of the Church are over. People are asking questions and making up their own minds about the answers. And some of the biggest questions they are asking are about God and how we relate to God. No longer can priests and ministers simply inform their congregations about these things as if they were hard facts, set in concrete forever. Their task now is surely to open up these matters, and encourage exploration in two directions: honest thinking and genuine spiritual experience.

The ultimate question, I guess, is what is the purpose of prayer? I'm not asking 'why do we do it?' because if it is true that it's hard-wired into us it is not just something we choose to do. But what is its biological purpose? What does it achieve for the human race?

For sure, it can have the effect of changing us ourselves. Even praying 'Please let me pass my exam' can result in our working harder for it because the praying has confirmed to us that we want very much to pass. Praying for guidance in a difficult situation can, by passing the problem to that something-greater outside ourselves, calm our minds and help us to sort out the options. Praying a blessing on a friend can make us act more warmly towards them.

This is not to say that the good effects of prayer are all explained away in humanist terms. Plenty of us in difficult times have known the mysterious sense of being upheld by the prayers of others – even when we didn't know they were praying for us until afterwards – and we always seem to use that significant word 'upheld'.

We pray almost instinctively for an end to war, hunger, drought, and for people unknown to us who are suffering from disasters in far-off countries. Maybe that praying changes our priorities, and through us changes the world. Maybe it simply swells up into that spirit of all that is, that 'something-greater', and spreads out re-creating goodness. How it works is a mystery. But deep down, most of us believe it does work.

32

Land of Saints and Survivors?

After her recent visit to Italy, the author asks if it is possible that Ireland is now the most Catholic country in Europe [25 April 2009]

Sometimes I wonder if Ireland is the most openly Catholic country left in Europe. In France, Portugal, even Poland, very little public evidence of religion remains. Forty or even thirty years ago, driving through France, we used to see wayside shrines at crossroads way out in the middle of nowhere, lovingly filled with fresh flowers by local people. Now they are almost extinct. In rural France now a visitor may have to travel some distance on a Sunday to find a parish church where Mass is said.

A couple of weeks ago we had an extended-family holiday in Tuscany in Italy.

I had never been to Italy except for three days in Venice some years ago. And Venice is such a magical fairytale place that I hardly thought of it as being part of Italy. So it was going to be good to see the real Italy.

It was a delight. The friendly people, the swirling landscape, the colourful buildings, the beautiful towns in this so very beautiful part of Italy. The first full day we were there was Palm Sunday. In the small nearby town we saw people coming away from the church carrying large fans of soft grey-green olive branches as they stopped to talk, or to sit at one of the many outdoor cafés. A lovely sight. But in the end, a rather sad one. The green branches were a visual marker of who had been to Mass and who hadn't. And clearly the Mass-goers were only a small minority.

Attempts to find out what was happening in the churches on the other days of Holy Week, leading up to Good Friday, were rarely successful. In one village there was to be a 9.30 pm Mass on Maundy Thursday, but then nothing until Easter Sunday. In another village it seemed there would be some sort of Good Friday procession at 9.30 pm, which seemed an odd time.

Someone asked me to get a picture of the Pope for a friend – in Italy, they said, that wouldn't be a problem. But I couldn't find any religious items in the shops. The one church that I saw with a shop inside it sold only the gaily coloured pottery ware of the region, and a few postcards. On a market stall opposite the leaning tower of Pisa, among the gaudy goods to tempt tourists, I saw one framed picture of Padre Pio and a twin picture of the Virgin Mary, both rather violently coloured. But that was all. No little corner shops such as we have in Ireland, with those gentle cream statuettes, that I so loved when I was small, of the Virgin and the saints. There were plenty of stalls outside the big city cathedrals, stalls of T-shirts and bags and mugs and every sort of tourist enticement – but no rosaries, no holy pictures.

Out in the country a few – really very few – wayside shrines, looking desperately neglected. In the cities, crumbling and discoloured remains of old ones high up on the walls.

Italy is not altogether bad news for God, though. In towns and villages most churches are open and people are free to walk in and wander around, stop for a quick prayer if they want to without anyone intruding. These churches are clean and well-cared for. Often there is a tape of sacred music playing quietly. Lacking a formal service on Good Friday this year, I observed it by just being still for a time, in a calm and simple church, with Bach's Matthew Passion playing softly in the background. I was not alone: a few people in work clothes or carrying shopping came in and out, to and from the confessional. That felt like a good Good Friday.

I shouldn't generalise about the state of religion in Italy on the basis of a week spent in one small and relatively wealthy region. All the same, the overall picture I got was that the country once so piously devout has simply sidelined piety and become as materialistic as any other place. Years ago, Italy and Ireland used to be described as the most Catholic countries in Europe. Later Poland was added to the list, and the word is that even that country is less openly religious than it was when its own Polish Pope was alive. So that leaves Ireland.

Are we still religious in Ireland? I think so. People sometimes still cross themselves when they pass a church. The Angelus is still rung from countless churches, and has its own slot on television, a few contemplative moments which even those of us who are not Catholic appreciate. You can say 'God bless you' when someone sneezes, and 'Thank God' when something good happens, without being considered weird. And somehow, oddly, it all makes for a sense of community, these casual displays of faith. A sense of being connected, within some sort of over-all care system. Disasters will happen, they will, but we are not left alone to cope with them.

One day last week, on the RTE Radio 1 *Today* programme, the scientist James Lovelock said an amazing thing. He was talking about the future of the world and of the human race. He believes that, because of global warming and over-population, 80% of humans will perish by the year 2100. He reckons that the climate change we are only beginning to see will mean that much of the world's land areas will become uninhabitable, with most of Europe becoming desert. Previously he has said that Britain will become Europe's 'life-raft', due to its stable temperature which comes from being surrounded by ocean. But last week, on RTE radio, he said that Ireland is probably the best country of all for survival. Less crowded than Britain, and with even more temperate weather — less hot in summer, less cold in winter.

So there you have it – maybe. Ireland the most openly religious country, Ireland the best country for physical survival? Put the two together and make of it what you will.

33

Good Can Surely Come Out of the Ryan Report

As Ireland reels at the shocking child abuse revelations contained in the recent Ryan report, the author hopes for a fresh start [6 June 2009]

'The stuff of nightmares.' 'The Irish Holocaust.' 'A crisis for Ireland.' Ever since the Ryan report came out we have not been able to stop talking about the terrible history of abuse of children that it has revealed. Turn on the radio and there's a discussion going on about it. Open a newspaper and every columnist and commentator is writing about it. Families talk about it, friends talk about it and even total strangers ask each other what they think about it. Ireland is in deep shock.

One response is to puzzle over what sort of culture there was in those times which made possible such horrific cruelty to small children and young people. It seems to have been a combination of centuries of repression by a foreign nation and, maybe as a direct result, a desire to place 'godly'

Irish people on a pedestal and treat them as though they themselves were small gods.

When my family and I moved to Ireland, thirteen years ago, we were astonished by the way some Catholic clergy (not all of them) expected to have everything done for them, as if the people were their servants. They did not seem to expect to wait their turn in a queue, or to have to pay for things the way ordinary human beings did. I have to admit, as a Church of Ireland clergyperson, that it was touching that clergy of other denominations were in some places given the same sort of queue-jumping priorities. That politeness always seemed a nice bit of ecumenism, even when it didn't feel right to take advantage of it.

Respect for clergy and for men and women in religious orders is fine. But here in Ireland, historically, it went beyond respect into an area where anything they did was to be respected and nothing they did was to be criticised.

Remember 'brain-washing'? That used to be something we associated with wars in the Far East, and then with strange religious cults, mostly in countries like America. Brain-washing in that sense meant that the followers of a particular leader or cult would do what ever they had been trained to do without any judgement of their own. Without allowing themselves to think whether what they were asked to do was right or wrong. The habit of obedience within the religious orders ('poverty, chastity and obedience') appears to have been so strong, during the last century at least, that it can only be described as brain-washing. We now know that nuns and monks (it is difficult in these circumstances to call them brothers and sisters) often maltreated the children

in their care not by their own decisions but because they
were told to by their superiors. The religious themselves
were brain-washed about their own behaviour and the people were brain-washed not to allow themselves see what the
religious were doing.

Now it is all, or nearly all, out in the open. These must be
the darkest days of the spirit of Ireland. The other dark days
of the past, years of famine and oppression, have been the
result of what nature and foreign power combined to inflict
on this country. But these horrors grew up among the generations of our parents and grandparents. They themselves
may not have abused the young but far too many of them
knew about such abuse and did not speak out against it.

Yet good can surely come out of all this. These revelations mean that our eyes can no longer stay conveniently
shut to the presence of evil. 'Say nothing' may have been a
necessary way of living when the oppressors were just
around every corner. But it will not do now in situations
where wrong is being done not by 'them' but among ourselves. And not just in the church but in every level of public
life. Why do we continue to joke about 'brown envelopes'
changing hands when someone wants something done that is
not legally available to them? Why do we persist in admiring
the 'cute whoors'? A couple of years ago some survey told
us that Ireland is the second most corrupt country in
Europe. The most corrupt was that other very Catholic
country, Italy. What is it about our moral teaching that has
allowed so many of us engage in corrupt practices, and so
many of the rest of us to admire it or at least to wink at it?

To joke about brown envelopes and cute whoors is to assume that nothing can be done about them. But indeed it can, if we realise we are tired of being robbed and rubbished, and if we object with loud enough voices. The Ryan report has caused such shock that it must be a call to us to sweep our whole house clean, clear it out, scrub it, make a fresh start. In politics and in our organisations and in government at local and national levels.

And in our churches, all our churches. Way off in the future I hope that people will be saying that the Ryan report was the turning point for Christianity in Ireland. That from 2009 onwards, authority has not been self-awarded but earned. That those who become the religious leaders in the community and in the country as a whole are chosen by the people themselves. That it is the people themselves who decide who will be their priests (including married men, and women, if that is what the people want) and who will be their bishops – if bishops are wanted. That it is the people who organise the churches, and that the leaders are not little princes but, following the teachings of Jesus, their servants.

Many people are convinced that the twenty-first century is a time of huge religious upheaval worldwide, an upheaval that seems to come every 500 years. Like the split between the Celtic church and the Roman church, then the split between the Orthodox church and the Roman Catholic Church, and then the Reformation. They believe that we are now on the verge of a totally renewed Christianity. Many others also believe that when God is totally exasperated with what people are doing she or he pulls the rug out from under them so it all has to start from scratch again. That would be wonderful.

34

Stopped in Our Tracks and Turned Around

The author thinks there are enough Christians to save the planet if they faced up to climate change [4 July 2009]

The church was gloomy, and there were not many people gathered together that Sunday morning. One or
two chatted in small huddles before the service began, but
the rest were scattered about the large building in lonely
ones or twos. The minister laboured valiantly through the
service with the congregation seeming like idle onlookers.
The prayers, the readings, the sermon and even the hymns
were delivered in a penitential drone, and at last it was all
over and we could escape into the fresh air.

Leaving the church, I turned off the road and in a few
moments I was walking through green shade, water sounds,
birdsong. All my senses came alive and I was lifted out of the
hour's gloom and into a sense of the wonder and glory of
life and nature and God.

There is an old-fashioned poem, *Garden Thoughts* by
Dorothy Frances Gurney, that says:

The kiss of the sun for pardon,
The song of the birds for mirth,
One is nearer God's heart in a garden
Than anywhere else on earth.

That's sometimes quoted by people in defence of not going to church. You can see what they're getting at. If you can meet God in nature why bother going to church?

The weak spot in that argument is that this is only part of the story. Churchgoing is about a lot more than our own personal feel-good contact with the divine. It's about our relationships with each other and with the world. It's about being shocked sometimes at where we're at. Stopped in our tracks and turned around. Our response to readings from the Gospels or the Old Testament may sometimes be, 'That's very nice,' but more often, if we're really listening to them, we hear a call to a bigger, better, braver life.

Getting all religious in a garden is fine, but then we are either on our own or with one or more other people we have chosen to be with. In church, on the other hand, we are brought into contact, without any choice, with all those 'neighbours' that Jesus talked about. 'Love God, and love your neighbour,' he said (having learnt it himself from the Hebrew scriptures). He reckoned those were the most important of all the religious laws. And those people in church are the neighbours. They are a mini-version of the wide world, of the millions and trillions of neighbours we will never meet. Some of them in far distant countries, some of them starving, some of them living in squalor, some of them dying of Aids. And we're supposed to love them? Do something about their problems?

The answer to that is not only Yes, that's what Jesus was saying, but also that by being grouped together in our churches we are in an ideal position to do so. We have such potential strength, with our huge numbers, to change the world that it is stunning if we think about it. So far we haven't really recognised the scope of our power. We use it for small things: the occasional charity event, a special collection here and there, and sometimes a pronouncement from our high-ups about the state of the world. For God's sake, why aren't we thinking bigger?

About climate change, for a start. What couldn't we do if we really faced up to it? Those who work on increasing our consciousness of what is happening to the planet say they have the choice of either downplaying it or causing widespread panic. Some dare to say that if a halt to climate change is not effected in three years the planet is doomed. If we have any sense that the world is God-given (whatever each of us means by that word 'God'), shouldn't we be putting all our energies into saving it from total ruin? Politicians on the whole won't do it because they think the necessary actions would cost them votes. Small groups here and there do what they can. Yet the churches, who might well consider themselves to have a duty to guard what God has created, are numerically much greater than all these small groups put together. It's true, they are doing more and more these days in the way of conferences and resolutions concerning the dangers of global warming and what we should be doing. But is that all? Those things will gradually increase the numbers of those who recognise what is happening, but they are not going to cause the wholesale changes that will save the world. Something much bigger is required.

Alastair McIntosh, in his very readable book *Hell and High Water: Climate Change, Hope and the Human Condition*

(Birlinn, 2008), says that it is spiritual starvation over two
centuries which has led to the riot of materialism and consumerism and greed which in turn has brought the planet to
the perilous state it is now in. He suggests, only half-jokingly,
a warning that should be put not just on cigarettes but on
consumer items in general: 'This product can seriously damage your planet causing loss of life and species extinction.'
How to tackle global warming, he says, is by technical, economic and political means, but first of all it is about how the
human soul can be re-instated.

He says: 'Alongside faith (which is to say, trusting perse-
verance), and charity (which is to say, love made manifest),
hope is one of the three cardinal virtues of the spiritual life.
That is what makes it so important that public discourse and
action on climate change is harnessed to a rekindling of the
inner life. Only then can we face death's dark vale and get
bearings with which to navigate Hell and High Water.'

Rekindling our spiritual lives in order to save the planet.
If Christians all over Ireland, all over the world, could set
aside our parochial preoccupations and, together, put all our
physical and spiritual energies and the huge power of our
numbers into these actions, there is no limit to what we
could achieve. No other worldwide organisation has such
potential power for good. In such work surely we would
find our true – and united – vocation.

35

Christian Unity from
the Grassroots

*The author encourages people on the ground to make
Christian unity happen rather than waiting for word from
the top [20 June 2009]*

My father was a Presbyterian on Sunday mornings and a Congregationalist in the afternoons. That was in his boyhood days in rural Wales. When he moved to the London suburbs he became a Methodist. It was all to do with what churches were nearby, and when their services were. I'm sure he thought God didn't mind which one he went to.

My mother was Roman Catholic because her whole family was Catholic, right back into the centuries of the bogs of Galway and Mayo. Right through generations of emigration to New York, and through her own meeting and marrying that Welshman in New York, and having children and moving to England, Canada, Wales, London ...

My siblings and I were brought up as Catholics. My father had had to swear that we would be, and he had no problem with that. There were family prayers, all of us gathered together in the kitchen before the youngest one went to bed. We girls went to convent schools, and our brother to one run by monks. And Dad wasn't going to let us slack on our religious duties. 'Have you been to Confession?' he'd sometimes ask on a Saturday, and 'Hurry up or you'll be late for Mass,' he'd maybe say on a Sunday.

Out of all that I became an Anglican priest. In the Church of England and then, beginning thirteen years ago, in the Church of Ireland. It was a long journey in between my childhood faith and my adult faith. It involved the throwing off of second-hand religion in my teens, followed by years of not-knowing, and then the wonder of discovering it all afresh when I was about thirty. It just happened that when I made that discovery the nearest Catholic church was many miles away and I had no car, and the church in the village where we lived was Anglican. So at the age of 29 I became an Anglican. Twenty years later I was ordained, and in 1994 was one of the first 880 women to become priests in the Church of England.

I love the Anglican Church. I love the breadth of it, the way worship can be 'low' (plain) or 'high' (fancy) and still be Anglican. I love the encouragement of thinking, and discussion, but also of silence and contemplation. I love the beautiful words of the old liturgy, and the earnest work done on newer forms of it. I love the importance placed on music and the visual arts in worship, and sometimes I miss that in the Church of Ireland, where Anglicanism is mostly low and unadorned.

I also love the Catholic Church. I love the simplicity of the Mass. I love the way the prayers which are said by the people need no books in hand, so that the praying comes through the heart, not the head. I love interiors of most Catholic churches in Ireland and Britain, full of light and softly coloured. (But I also love the intense darkness that

stuns you when you walk into many churches on the Conti-
nent.) Above all I love the way faith seems so naturally to
touch daily life for so many Catholics.

I also like the Quakers and the Unitarians and the Methodists, although my contact with them has been more limited. But I have often been uplifted by their services, and
moved by the sense of community that shines out from
them. Because in all of these churches and denominations
the bottom line, it seems to me, is the strength of community that grows where people meet regularly to pray and
worship and do good works together.

Increasingly, as I get older, I am impatient with the barriers between the churches, especially on a personal level.
Why should we only go to the church services of the church
we 'belong' to? Why shouldn't we be Catholic *and* Protestant, or Anglican *and* Quaker, or Methodist *and* Catholic?

When ecumenism was the big thing – twenty, thirty,
years ago – we waited breathlessly for our churches to unite
and become 'the one, holy, catholic church' (small 'c') that
we say in our Creeds that we believe in. A universal, undi-
vided church. But the years went by, and the practical difficulties seemed to increase, and the theological difficulties
were flying about all over the place. And gradually we realised that it wasn't going to happen in the simple and easy
way we had so foolishly imagined. Perhaps the people at the
top of the church establishments – popes and archbishops –
feel there is too much to lose. Perhaps, in getting to the top,
they have had to become so very cautious that they are
simply not the people to do it.

That leaves us, the people. We are always being told that we are the Church. If ecumenism cannot come from the top, let it come from the bottom, from the grassroots. We could blow away the old barriers if each of us belonged to more than one church.

The days of tribalism are surely over, and so too are the days when people were nervous of the men with the power of the Church. Instead we are in days of disillusionment with the old ways. Now the power lies with us, including the power for uniting our churches.

Thirteen years ago, when people asked me why I was leaving a lovely parish in England to come and work in Ireland, I said it was because I had the feeling that Christian unity was going to come into being first of all in Ireland, and I wanted to be there when it happened. Then I got here, and I wasn't so sure. Under the surface, I realised, there was a lot of 'us and them' feeling.

But a great deal has happened to our churches in thirteen years. Scandals, and falling numbers, loss of income, changes in ideas of ministry. Now, I think, we – perhaps especially the women – could do the ecumenism thing. Without waiting for the word from the top, just walking out there and doing it.

36

New Concepts which Will Allow Faith and Worship to Flourish[†]

Canon Hilary Wakeman reflects on the crisis in the
churches and a 'new Christianity', about which we must
talk openly [7 May 2002]

Most people believe in God. Most people pray, at least sometimes. Yet the Christian Church is dying.

Part of this is a general lack of enthusiasm for belonging to any organisation. Part of it is a disenchantment with hierarchical, authoritarian or sexist structures. But at the root of the decline is a change in belief about God. And almost nobody is talking about it.

A crisis in the churches, Catholic and Protestant, is boiling up underground and is beginning to break through here and there. The imminent 'heresy trial' of the Church of Ireland's Dean of Clonmacnoise is one of the eruptions. It shows clearly that the crisis is about the difference between intellectual expressions of faith and more intuitive ways of expressing it.

It is with the intuitive right side of the brain that people experience God – which is why so many find they are nearer to God in nature. It is with the right-brain that we appreci-

---

† Published in the 'Rite and Reason' column of the *Irish Times* on 7 May 2002

ate beautiful cathedrals, religious art and music. Yet organised worship is left-brain fodder, rational and wordy – prayers, readings, creeds, homilies.

'By love God may be caught and held; by thinking, never,' says the anonymous fourteenth century writer of *The Cloud of Unknowing*. Here is the crux of the matter: all credal statements about God have come from the analytical side of the human brain, and with that left-side they are now heard by churchgoers and church-refusers alike. Yet the impulse to make those statements must have come originally from right-side experiences of the reality of God.

Over past decades many writers, preachers and teachers have been signalling the need for new thinking. Many clergy and laypeople have privately adapted what they were taught; and go on playing 'The Emperor's New Clothes'. For the sake of others, or for material security, they 'see' what in truth they know is not there. There is a loss of integrity and, for some, feelings of guilt. Faith and worship cannot flourish in such a climate.

The way through all of this must surely be to find new ways of stating the old truths. To find what they were really expressing 2,000 years ago, and re-express them in ways not untrue to our present understanding. It is concepts such as the divinity of Jesus, the Fall, Atonement and Resurrection that stop rational and educated people from signing up to Christianity. By clinging to 2,000-year-old concepts – which we do in no other area of our lives – the Church deters people from becoming followers of Christ and part of a God-centred community.

The prime concept is the divinity of Jesus Christ. To say that 'Jesus is God' is a left-brain, concrete statement. Divine, full stop. Black/white: yes or no? true or untrue? To rationalists, not possible. But looking from the right-side we might say: there is something of God in every human being; in some people there is a lot of God; in Jesus there was so much of God that his followers couldn't see where Jesus ended and God began. So the word 'divine' began to be used of him.

Talk of 'the Third Person of the Trinity' is left-brain thinking: solid imagery, a person. It is difficult not to visualise him/her/it as another being in a nightie. But seen from the intuitive right-side, 'God's spirit' is not one of three People inside God but another way of saying 'God's influence'.

All those other rigid, rationally worked out concepts – the Resurrection, the Atonement, the authority of the scriptures, sin and forgiveness – all can be read in a new way consonant with our present knowledge of ourselves and our world. They can be expressed with integrity, not going against reason but giving value to that which lies beyond mere reasoning, in the realm of art and poetry and intuition.

If these ancient formulations can be let go, and we can allow God be greater than anything we can control with our thinking, then Christians will be truly the monotheists we think we are but have not been. We can get back to the God that Jesus knew, and taught others to know. We will still be Christians, as followers of the teachings and example of Jesus, the Christ, 'the anointed one'. We can be in touch with his spirit because it is part of us and can be related to, just as the spirit of a beloved friend is part of us beyond

their death. We can continue to share bread and wine together in remembrance of him, and know his presence in
that commemoration. Other sacraments, liturgies, scriptures
will come alive because we will be contacting them out of a
fresh sense of truth, not with our fingers crossed behind our
backs. Christianity will live.

But first we need to talk openly and honestly with each
other.

37

Theological Myths at Root of Church's Decline[‡]

*Has much of Christianity become a case of
believing the unbelievable? [22 December 2003]*

'There are parts of the Creed that I don't actually believe, but I like saying it,' a young man said at a recent
gathering. I am beginning to think that what he said is a clue
to what is happening in all our churches, Catholic and Protestant. It could be showing us what lies at the root of the
decline of Christianity.

Two thousand years ago there lived a man called Jesus
whose teachings altered the history of the world. His own

‡ Published in the 'Rite & Reason' column of *The Irish Times*, 22 December
2003

personal godliness gave those teachings power, and made
them live into the centuries ahead. But after his death the
story of his life was mythologised by his followers, as so often happened in those times. The followers themselves became the building blocks of a vast institution. When disputes
arose, particularly concerning the nature of Jesus – just how
godly was he? – then the church authorities, and even secular authorities like the Emperor Constantine, wrote out
formulations of belief to which all Christians were required
to assent. This was a time when the earth was thought to be
flat, and heaven and hell to be actual geographical places
above and below the earth. Naturally, the beliefs about Jesus
fitted into that understanding of the world. Jesus was said to
have come down from heaven, and ascended into it again. As
our understanding of the universe grew, our theological
statements were left behind. As late as 1950 the then Pope
was defining as an Article of Faith the idea that Jesus's
mother Mary was 'assumed' into heaven after her death, that
her actual flesh and bones were taken into heaven and re-
united with her soul. As the scientist Richard Dawkins has
pointed out, 'What can that mean, if not that Heaven is a
physical place, physical enough to contain bodies?'

That is just one small example of the way our theological
statements have got stuck in the past. And people are re-
jecting them. Often they struggle for years with the dishonesty of standing in church Sunday by Sunday and proclaiming
things they know are not true: that Jesus began life without a
human father, and ended it without a normal death; that he
was not only human like the rest of us but was also made of
the same material as the (non-material) God. They struggle,

and try not to think or talk about it all, and then leave the Church, often sadly. Outsiders, faced with apparently having to take ancient myth and metaphor as literal twenty-first century truth, do not come into the Church. And we do not talk about any of this.

The young man with whose remark I began this piece probably represents a far greater proportion of Christians than he realises. How many of us have for years felt vaguely guilty at saying words we do not really, heart of hearts, believe, but have gone on saying them because they sound beautiful, and comfort and uphold us when we say them? The loss of the old Latin Mass is still felt keenly by many Catholics, just as many Church of Ireland people prefer the sixteenth century language of the old Prayer Book services, even those parts where the theology is barbaric. In both cases, the music of the language carries us into the intuitive part of our brain, as stained glass windows and incense do. In that intuitive, right-brain mode we feel closer to God than when we say the prosaic words of the modern services.

So this is what I think is happening: we are accepting out-of-date doctrine because it sounds good and feels good when we say it as Creed or prayer. But underneath our comfort lies an unacknowledged sense of dishonesty, that all the time is laying the hand of death on the Church. How do we resolve this?

Above all, we will have to be truthful. We will need to admit to each other, and to outsiders, that the words we say do not have to be taken literally, but are often the sort of poetry and paradox that let us into a non-rational perception of the divine. We will need to admit that as long as we are limited-range humans there is no one Truth to which we can all assent. But we can each try to discover what is genuinely true for us, at each stage of our life; and allow other followers of Christ to do the same, just as we allow Jews and Muslims, Hindus and Buddhists their own understanding of the divine.

With new-found integrity, our faith in God will be free to grow. Our devotion to the figure of Jesus and his teachings, and our sense of the presence in us of 'the mind that was in Christ', will be free to grow. It is a tremendous prospect. God be with us.

38

What Next for Christianity in Ireland?[§]

The author asks, is Christianity in Ireland slowly dwindling away or is it moving into recovery mode after a few bad years? [11 September 2006]

What is going on in the churches in Ireland? What is happening in the parishes? Does anyone really know? Is Christianity slowly dwindling away, or is it moving into recovery mode after a few bad years? Or are the num-

---

[§] Published in the 'Rite and Reason, column of *The Irish Times*, 11 September 2006

bers of churchgoers actually increasing, as some have claimed?

We don't do much in the way of surveys in Ireland, so it is difficult to know the answer. A young boy from Dublin came into a Church of Ireland service in the rural West recently and asked 'Is it usually this empty?' His home church is so full every Sunday that the number of services have had to be doubled. But which church gives the truer picture of the state of Irish Anglicanism in the twenty-first century?

A year or two ago we were hearing that the abuse scandals in the Catholic Church in Ireland were causing thousands to drop away from the faith. In a rare survey, conducted last year by Milltown Brown IMS, we learnt that almost two-thirds of Catholics had lost their trust in the clergy. The Archbishop of Dublin has said that in many city congregations there were no young people at all between the ages of 16 and 36. And with almost half of the 16,000 Catholic clergy now aged between 50 and 70, and only 19 ordinations last year, dioceses are beginning to think of amalgamating parishes.

Richard Holloway, former Anglican Bishop of Edinburgh, who will be speaking in Dublin this week, says he has given up trying to prophesy what will happen to Christianity. He sees religion currently as being in four strands. The first is what some people call fundamentalism, but he prefers to call 'strong' religion: the sort of faith that insulates itself from the world and goes on asserting the old ways and beliefs. It is easy to see its attractiveness in an insecure world. The second he calls, without being derogatory, 'weak' religion, perhaps typified by the Anglican Church, which has tried to adapt its theology and spirituality to be sensitive to what is happening in society. It wants to be loyal to its religious tradition while taking account of current thinking about such things as equality, structures, science. The third group are the people who have moved from 'weak' religion to post-religion. Unable to buy the whole doctrinal package, they hold to the best of the religious tradition, in music and art and worship. They are practising but non-believing Christians. And finally there are those who find all talk of God bewilderingly absurd: these are the truly secular.

'Strong' religion will probably continue to flourish, he thinks, letting Christianity in for a difficult time. What will become of the second and third groups he doesn't know. The Pope, who he thinks is a wise man, talks of battening down the hatches and weathering the storm. Holloway, who is the former Primus of the Scottish Episcopal Church, disagrees.

'I would rather enter into dialogue with the world – because we are all in the world. Personally I welcome the excitement of all this. If humanity survives, religion could be the means of us all living in peace with one another – even though it isn't doing that at present.'

The Open Christianity Network, which has invited Richard Holloway to speak, is made up mostly of people from the second and third groups. The purpose of its meetings in Dublin, Cork, and the North is to provide spaces where ideas about faith and tradition, and about church structures, can be freely and confidentially explored with others, without leadership.

What Richard Holloway finds most worrying about the current state of Christianity is its leaders. 'They get into a kind of institutional ethic. There are people who like institutions. They set them up, they run them. But what happens to the main vision? The people in charge of the institutions are mechanics. They lose sight of what the journey is for, and all they care about is preserving the vehicle. The worldwide Anglican Church, in its difficulties over homosexuality, is obsessed with preserving the vehicle. But it would no longer pass the NCT. Maybe we need a new method of transportation.'

'The biggest joy in the present state of things is the appetite in good human beings for non-institutional spirituality – they have been called 'devout sceptics'.' He is currently doing a television programme about art and religion, and is fascinated by the effect on the very secular crew of great works of art. 'I am not talking religion at them, but they are picking up a sense of Otherness.' Institutional religion, he adds, has no monopoly on human beings.